Estimating Marketed Surplus in Gujarat Agriculture

About the Author

Munish Alagh is Senior Fellow of the Indian Council of Social Science Research (ICSSR) at the Sardar Patel Institute of Economic and Social Research (SPIESR) in Ahmedabad, Gujarat. He has authored more than 10 publications in reputed journals of Economics. He has authored two books on agricultural economics and entrepreneurship, respectively in 2011 and 2015. He has held teaching positions in different institutions in Ahmedabad from 1999 to 2010. He was awarded the Chimanbhai Patel Award for the Best Research Paper among teachers of the Gujarat University in 2004. Dr Alagh holds a doctoral degree from Mumbai University (2007).

Estimating Marketed Surplus in Gujarat Agriculture

New Vistas Explored

MUNISH ALAGH

ACADEMIC FOUNDATION
NEW DELHI

www.academicfoundation.org

First published in 2016
by

ACADEMIC FOUNDATION
4772-73 / 23 Bharat Ram Road, (23 Ansari Road),
Darya Ganj, New Delhi - 110 002 (India).
Phones : 23245001 / 02 / 03 / 04.
Fax : +91-11-23245005.
E-mail : books@academicfoundation.com
www.academicfoundation.org

Disclaimer:
The opinions/views/findings expressed in this book are solely those of the author and do not necessarily reflect the views of the publisher.

Cataloging in Publication Data--DK
Courtesy: D.K. Agencies (P) Ltd. <docinfo@dkagencies.com>

Alagh, Munish, author.
Estimating marketed surplus in Gujarat agriculture : new vistas explored / Munish Alagh.
pages cm
Includes bibliographical references.
ISBN 9789332703568

1. Surplus agricultural commodities--India--Gujarat. 2. Agriculture--Economic aspects--India--Gujarat. I. Title.

HD9016.I43G85 2016 DDC 338.1095475 23

Typeset, printed and bound by The Book Mint, New Delhi.
www.thebookmint.in

Contents

List of Tables

Tables

Acknowledgements

This study "Estimating Marketed Surplus in Gujarat Agriculture: New Vistas Explored" was sponsored by the Ministry of Agriculture, Government of India, New Delhi. I am thankful to the Ministry.

I would like to acknowledge Centre for Management in Agriculture (CMA), Indian Institute of Management (IIM), Ahmedabad, which appointed me as post-doctoral fellow on the study and Prof Vasant Gandhi, Chairperson, CMA, who has given me permission to publish the report. I would also like to thank Prof Sukhpal Singh (CMA) and Prof Vijay Paul Sharma (CMA) for guiding me through the project.

I would also like to place on record my thanks to Mr Ashwin Rawal, Mr Y.V. Pantulu, Mr Nishaad Rao and Mr Ramesh Maaji for data collection, tabulation and computer assistance. I thank the librarian and staff of the Vikram Sarabhai Library and the staff of the Publications Division of IIM, Ahmedabad, for providing support whenever required.

— Munish Alagh

Preface

> While it is true that with the opening of the economy, farmer-market linkages for the rural economy have become more effective. The question is has market agriculture in Gujarat more effectively established the state of the *gujarati* Farmer? This is the Million Dollar Question.
>
> —Munish Alagh, Senior Fellow, ICSSR.

Gujarat agriculture is market dominated, but the efficiency of the market, and specifically institutions and inputs in Gujarat agriculture is still open to question. Many authors (Patnaik, and Shah, 2013; Dixit, 2009; Kumar et al., 2010; Dholakia and Datta, 2010, Shah et al., 2009) have commented on agriculture and agricultural growth in Gujarat, and others have debated ad nauseam about the controversy of whether or not there has been high all round growth in Gujarat. On this second matter, for an authoritative comment and overview of the debate see Ravindra Dholakia's paper in May 2014 in the *Economic and Political Weekly* (Dholakia, 2014). Here we do not get into this larger debate, instead we look at specific variables connected with this issue to get to the crux of the matter in question, within this broad theme we focus our analysis on the question of how effective agricultural institutions have been to transform agricultural market in Gujarat. We then empirically supplement our analysis with some findings from our Research Report conducted at Indian Institute of Management.

The main objectives of the study were to estimate marketable and marketed surplus of selected food grains in Gujarat and to examine the role of institutional, infrastructural and socio-economic factors in influencing household marketed surplus decisions. Wheat, *bajra* and *tur* were covered. The study covered five districts Vadodara, Panchmahals, Kheda, Junagadh and Banaskantha. Totally 359 farmers were surveyed.

The study revealed that marketed surplus output ratio was on the lower side because the farmer always insures minimum amount of (approximately 30%) output for self-consumption.

If storage, seeds and pest removal is stepped up and the farmer is given even greater support by more enthusiastic government machinery and officers, the food security of the farmers can increase. This is the only way the retention proportion of Gujarati farmers can be reduced, but this is a slow process, it will take decades not years.

Earlier studies had different results i.e., a lower marketed surplus ratio for foodgrains like wheat and *bajra*. The onset of liberalisation may not have led to greater emphasis on agriculture but has definitely led to a greater emphasis on the market as our results show.

To set the general stage for this study: Gujarat agriculture is the flavour of the day, if one was to read the newspapers recently with Gulati, Alagh et al., all giving different views. Identifying strengths and weaknesses, with increased speed of economic policy reforms in the post 1991-92 period, Gujarat improved in its growth performance remarkably. In fact as Ravindra Dholakia in his articles often states, if growth acceleration in the post 1991-92 period is attributed to economic policy reforms at the national level, it is obvious that Gujarat has benefited from such reforms much more than other states. However as any Masters student of Modern Growth Theory will tell you, innovation and ideas are more important than just investment or technology in the nuanced paradigm of development thinking nowadays.

Emphasis on development of commercial crops in the state had not resulted in higher incomes in the agricultural sector itself. The share of the primary sector in state GDP (gross domestic product) had fallen to 19 per cent by 1999-2000 and this low proportion continued thereafter. This is a result of a decline in the absolute level of real agricultural output in the years following 1999-2000 and a simultaneous increase in output in the secondary and tertiary sectors. Prices have moved in favour of the agricultural sector. However, per capita income in the primary sector has always been the lowest of all three sectors. The agricultural sector has served to fuel economic growth in other sectors, but that economic growth has not fed into the sector itself.

Ravindra Dholakia, Ashok Gulati, Samar Datta and Tushaar Shah among others have praised Gujarat agriculture for efficiency in public investment, supporting irrigation etc. Niti Mehta, Anita Dixit, Amita Shah et al., have raised distributive concerns. The price factor specifically rising agricultural price ratio is not given sufficient emphasis but instead is simply used as a limitation in the context of inequality when linked with declining per worker income level. But, there is more to be learnt from price responsiveness as I have brought out in my articles in *Economic and Political Weekly* and my thesis published by Academic Foundation. Sebastian Morris in a recent critique of my book on agricultural prices talks about an agricultural development model which is relevant in this context, he mentions that if in a particular area (like Gujarat for instance) the agricultural economy is dominated by peasant farms who maximise value added minus purchased inputs, and there is little or no disguised unemployment and the market wages are too high to support agriculture at the national level prices (so that the farmer needs a sufficient working agriculture market and a price responsive agriculture to have incentive to till the land on his own and invest in a lot of agricultural machinery). Now in such an area, and in an open economy, imports through the demand side can affect output, also the presence of capitalist farms opens up the issue. The Indian policy makers' stock response to such a situation is for Krushi Mahotsavs to help shore up the farmer, which purports to increase his efficiency but in fact provides very little substance. The stock in trade issues raised by economists working on Gujarat are efficiency in public investment, seeds and fertilisers and irrigation, or even distributive concerns go only so far, you need an efficient Government supporting a well functioning market.

A lot of publicity is given for instance about the impact of Sardar Sarovar in Gujarat. However in my field visits I found that even though large farmers having electric tube wells in Kheda and Baroda falling in catchment areas have become more prosperous and their situation has also improved due to excess flood waters and catchment area of Mahi Canal in these two districts, as far as the rest is concerned, for instance Saurashtra and Rocky areas of Panchmahals, Narmada impact is not yet felt so we can say actual impact of Narmada project right now is limited to a few areas.

I found the counter-factual to an approach focussing mainly on public investment in my field trips: a Patel wheat farmer in Kheda district in Gujarat, he is a farmer who has a large number of his family living in the United States, he operates his large plot with three huge mechanised tractors and migrant labour, if it is available at an affordable rate which it increasingly is not. He is not going to develop with doles through Krushi Mahotsavs. He needs a functioning agricultural market supported by Government marketing machinery which buys up his large production at remunerative prices. Until his stock is sold off at a remunerative rate, he does not get much benefit from farming through the year or even by remaining in India in contrast to the rest of his family. Meanwhile unless the Government Marketing and Storing facilities are performing efficiently and the stocks are being purchased sold and then being utilised efficiently for domestic consumption as well as exports, he will not get a good rate the next year. No doubt a good monsoon does affect price support but a marketing mechanism, a stocking mechanism and a storing mechanism that supports the farmer is the need of the hour. For this the requirement is to keep the farmer at the forefront of farming policies followed by the government. Capitalist farms and unsystematic imports in a completely non-nuanced liberal capitalist model do not serve the needs of either the *gujarati* farmer or the Indian farmer. The farmer of 2014 is price responsive, but if you treat him using borrowed 'trickle down' models or alternatively capitalist commercialisation without understanding the nuances of the Indian market you will harm him.

Ramesh Chand writes in the *Indian Express (*16 March 2016) that since the 1970s the agricultural markets in India have not moved towards a competitive market. While it is true that with the opening of the economy since the 1980s, particularly since 1991, farmer-market linkages for the rural economy have become more effective; the rural economy is more interlinked. The question is have institutions and institutional factors moved in a way to make market agriculture in Gujarat more effectively networked and institutionally established in terms of the state of the *gujarati* farmer. This in the institutional economics sense is the million dollar question.

1

Introduction and Review

1.1 Introduction

1.1.1 The Backdrop

The available data on marketable and marketed surplus based on surveys conducted by the Directorate of Marketing and Inspection during earlier decades have become obsolete. There have been persistent demands from the users for revision and updating of the data not only on marketable surplus ratios, but also on variety of other crucial items like farm retention for family consumption, seed, feed and wastages etc. This information is extensively used by government departments, ministries and organisations like the Department of Statistics, Ministry of Planning and Department of Agriculture & Cooperation (DAC) in framing estimates of NNP (net national product) of agricultural sector, consumption, expenditure, savings, capital formation etc. This information is also used in long- and short-term supply and demand projections as well as for estimating availability of important commodities for consumption. The Ministry of Commerce and Industry uses the marketable surplus ratios for assigning weights to different agricultural commodities in compilation of "All India Index Numbers of Wholesale Prices". The marketable surplus ratios are also very useful for planning procurement operations and market development programs what is now called the agricultural supply chain. Besides, it is of immense help to researchers of various agricultural universities/institutions at national level, Food & Agriculture Organization of the United Nations (FAO) and other international organisations.

Gujarat is among one of the fastest growing states in India. During the 10th Five Year Plan the state grew annually at a rate of 10.4

per cent, official statistics reveal a high rate of agricultural growth since the early years of the new millennium averaging at 8.6 per cent per annum (Mehta, 2012b). In the 1990s and early part of the new millennium, Gujarat witnessed overall improvements in yields of important food crops, even though the cropping pattern gave way to commercial crops which are more remunerative to the farmers. Clearly in this fast growing agriculture, a necessary subject of research is the quantum and proportion of the marketed part of the total production of food grains in the state. In the following, we explore this factor in detail.

This introductory chapter includes a description of the methodology, concepts and literature review. The second chapter describes the States Agriculture. The third chapter contains the empirical findings and the final chapter summarises the major findings and conclusion.

1.1.2 Objectives of the Study

The main objectives of the study are:

1. To estimate marketable and marketed surplus of selected food grains in Gujarat.
2. To estimate farm retention for consumption, seed, feed, wages and other payments in kind, etc.
3. To examine the role of various institutional, infrastructural, socio-economic factors that influence households decision on marketed surplus.

1.1.3 Methodology and Coverage

The study covers districts with maximum production of the relevant crops, wheat, *bajra* and *tur*. At first stage five districts were chosen, Vadodara and Panchmahals for *tur*, Kheda for wheat and *bajra*, Junagadh for wheat and Banaskantha for *bajra*. Cultivator households from these districts were selected as per multi-stage sampling, first appropriate villages were selected through judgement sampling based on yield and production figures found from study of the records of the district agricultural office and then appropriate households were selected through quota sampling design based on farm size. The sampling involved selection of appropriate blocks and villages based on statistical data available from the district offices. Finally, village level detailed farming information relevant for estimating marketed surplus was obtained from survey at the village level. This included—sale price, productivity, machinery used, cropping pattern, irrigation mechanisms etc. Finally, farm-level ratios were collected from selected households through pre-tested questionnaire. The data was then tabulated and analysed.

Care was taken in selection of blocks, villages and households to ensure that blocks and villages were selected with higher production and yield of selected crop (according to data available at District Agricultural Office). Household selection was done keeping in mind proportion of farmers of different farm size required to be chosen.

A brief profile of the sample selected is given in Table 1.1.

Table 1.1

Sample Coverage of Farmers by Crop and District

Farm Class	*Tur*		*Wheat*			*Bajra*		*Total*
	Vadodara	*Panch-mahal*	*Junagadh*	*Kheda*	*Banas-kantha*	*Kheda*	*Banas-kantha*	
Marginal	1	2	0	0	0	2	0	5
Small	1	9	0	7	1	14	3	35
Medium	24	19	32	45	27	61	44	252
Large	24	19	47	15	18	22	31	176
Total	50	49	79	67	46	99	78	468

Note: Three hundred and fifty nine farmers were interviewed in all. In the case of wheat and *bajra* in Kheda and Banaskantha District the same farmer was interviewed twice.

Source: Sample Data.

1.1.4 Main Features of Agriculture in Selected Districts

Kheda

Kheda district is in Central Gujarat. There are 10 *talukas* and two sub-divisions in the district (Nadiad and Kapadwanj). Under Nadiad division the *talukas* are: Nadiad, Mahuda, Mahembdabad, Kheda and Matar. Under Kapadwanj division the *talukas* are: Kapadwanj, Kathlal, Balasinor, Virpur and Thasra. In Kapdwanj district, cropping pattern in *kharif* involves cultivation of *bajra* and *chikori*. *Chikori* is a very profitable crop. In Nadiad division, rice is the main crop grown in Matar and Kheda. In Kapadwanj division the main crop is *bajra*. Yield per hectare is high in this area. After *bajra* in summer, wheat is cultivated in *rabi* season, if irrigation facility is available. After Rice crop, farmers sow wheat because there is retained moisture and nitrogen in land. Tarapur and Nadiad are main markets for selling produce. The majority of farmers sell produce at the field to traders. Majority of the farmers retain the produce for self-consumption. Some portion of *bajra* is sold, whereas 100 per cent of the wheat crop is sold. They get higher price for summer *bajra* compared to *kharif bajra* due to difference in the quality. Farmers never stock *bajra* and wheat for later sale. Farmers need working capital for the next agricultural season, therefore sell a large part of production immediately in the market.

Table 1.2

Basic Profile of Sample Selected in the Project

District	*Vadodara*	*Panchmahal*	*Kheda*	*Junagadh*	*Banaskantha*
Total blocks	12	11	10	14	14
Blocks covered	Karjan	Halol	Nadiad	Junagadh	Palanpur
	Vadora	Kalol	Mahemdabad	Mendarada	Vadgam
	Vaghodia	Ghoghumba		Manavadar	Deesa
Villages covered	Mangrol	Vada Talav	Valetava	Majevadi	Palanpur
	Kumbola	Jepura	Vedtal	Goladhhar	Lunava
	Runvad	Bakrol	Narsanda	Mendrada	Saripada
	Ghoda	Shaktipura	Sihunj	Datrona	Malan
	Anroli		Jariya	Manavadar	Vadgam
Total village covered	5	4	5	5	6
Main crop covered	*Tur*	*Tur*	Wheat/*Bajra*	Wheat	*Bajra*
Total sample	50	50	101	80	78

Source: Sample Data.

Panchmahal

Panchmahal district has two sub-divisions i.e., Godhra and Lunawada. The cropping pattern in Panchmahal is mainly mixed cropping—maize and *tur*. They depend on rainfed cultivation. As far as *tur* is concerned, it is a six-month crop. After three months, green *tur* is available. Every 15 days they collect green *tur* from the farm and sell in the market and receive a comparatively higher market price. But the majority of farmers harvest green *tur* and sell it in the market. Some farmers are involved in interlinked markets and hence sell their produce to the local traders as repayment of the credit. Some farmers take green *tur* and sell in the market as they need the capital/working capital for the next season (for purchasing seed and fertiliser and other agricultural activities). Farmers insist that government declares market price at the time of sowing. However, the government's policy is to declare price at the time of production. Having taken the sowing and input application decisions, the farmers in adverse circumstances incur substantial losses.

In Panchmahal the main markets are Rameshra, Shivnagar and Halol. The majority of farmers sell 60-70 per cent of production in the market. Farmers also distribute *tur* to neighbours, labour working in the field and require some for other customary requirements.

Junagadh

Junagadh is a major wheat producing district in Gujarat. The main *rabi* crop in Junagadh is wheat. Although some farmers have tube wells, major source of irrigation is ordinary well. Yield per hectare is 4000-4500 kg. In *kharif* season, farmers produce groundnut and cotton. Some farmers produce cotton crop also. The produce is not retained because of unavailability of warehousing facility.

At the time of harvesting, the weight of wheat is more compared to wheat stored for long duration after production. Majority of the farmers sell their produce to local traders. The Food Corporation of India (FCI) buys production in limited quantity. Farmers do not directly sell to FCI because there is a belief that FCI representatives screen for product quality, and if the production is rejected, they receive less price. FCI also purchases from the local traders. In fact local traders reportedly make profits from buying from the farmers and selling to the FCI. They take advantage of the cash needs of the farmers.

Banaskantha

Banaskantha contributes significantly to agricultural production of the state and ranks at the top in the production of potatoes in India.

There are two sub-divisions of the director of agriculture office: (1) Palanpur and (2) Deesa. The main crop is *bajra* and potato is a cash crop. The highest yield of potato in Gujarat is in Banaskantha. For irrigation facility major sources are wells and tube wells. Joint tube well ownership among farmers is there in the district. In *kharif* season, farmers cultivate *bajra*, groundnut, *til* and cotton. In *rabi* season, the major crops are: potatoes, wheat, cumin and fodder. In summer season, the major crops are *bajra*, vegetable and fodder. The main occupation of the district is farming and animal husbandry is subsidiary. From animal husbandry, they earn around 40 per cent of the household income. Some farmers sell water from their deep tube wells. Farmers take advance from the local traders and sell agricultural production to them. Every week they sell potatoes in the local market. Agricultural Produce Marketing Committee (APMC) market (Deesa and Palanpur) is far away and majority of the farmers sell their produce at the fields. Farmers repeat the wheat seeds for two years.

Vadodara

Vadodra district has 12 blocks. Farmers get low price for their product. They do not get proper price in APMC market. Traders do not give price as per government support price. They often grow *tur* for self-consumption. They do not do contract farming. Farmers are aware about price of *tur* but they do not get proper price from traders on account of their cash needs and lack of storage facilities. Wild animals foraging farm lands is a big problem.

Table 1.3 presents the percentage share of highest ranked districts in terms of area, production and yield of the selected foodgrain crops i.e., *tur*, *bajra* and wheat in Gujarat. Junagadh is the highest ranking district in Gujarat in terms of area, production and yield of wheat. Banaskantha holds a similar position in *bajra* and Vadodara in *tur*.

1.2 Microeconomic Concepts for Marketed Surplus[1]

The literature on agricultural market analysis is full of heuristic papers, where the authors take factors they believe to be of importance

1. Pindyck, Robert and Daniel Rubinfeld (2009). *Microeconomics. Student Value Edition.* 7th Edition. Prentice Hall. pp.199-200.

and explain or use them as determining variables. A certain amount of description of the concepts behind production choices, cost of production, trade possibilities and factors determining them in theory and welfare aspects of trade may be useful in setting the field as it were. We begin with a preliminary description of the concepts to be used.

Table 1.3

District-wise Percentage Share of Area, Production and Yield of Wheat, Bajra and Tur of 3 Year Annual Average (December 2007, December 2008 and December 2009) in Gujarat

Districts	*Area (%)*	*Production (%)*	*Yield Kg/ha.*
	Wheat		
Junagadh	14.3	19.43	3607.33
Ahmedabad	11.9	7.41	3557.67
Rajkot	7.6	10.24	3319
Kheda	5.9	5.60	2873.67
Banaskantha	5.8	5.57	2904.67
	Bajra		
Banaskantha	29.3	23.3	1025
Kheda	7.9	8.3	1706.67
Mahesana	7.7	7.7	1697.33
	Tur		
Vadodara	26.6	29.6	1443.67
Bharuch	16.6	13.02	1208.33
Panchmahals	10.1	15.83	1033.67

Source: Centre for Monitoring Indian Economy Pvt. Ltd. (CMIE).

The basic underlying theory which we need to focus on in the study of marketed surplus includes:

1. The relation between production of the foodgrain crops and the inputs required for them.
2. The nature of the market supply functions in an agricultural market.
3. Effect of government policies like MSP (minimum support policy) on the market for foodgrains specifically welfare implications.

4. Backward bending labour supply curves under certain conditions.

We divide our study into two sections.

1.2.1 Partial Equilibrium Analysis

The concept we first take into consideration is the Product Transformation Curve.

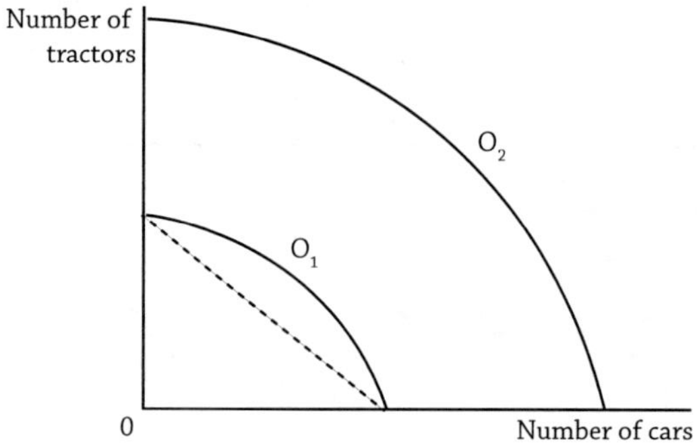

To study the economic advantages of joint production, let's consider a farm that produces two crops, wheat and *bajra*. Both crops use capital (equipment and livestock assets) and labour inputs. Wheat and *bajra* are not typically produced in the same land, but they do share farming resources, and both rely on similar machinery equipment (like tractors, etc) and labourers. The farmer must choose how much of each crop to produce. We have two product transformation curves, each showing the various combinations of wheat and *bajra* that can be produced with a given input of farm labourers and machinery. The inside curve describes all combinations of the two outputs that can be produced with a relatively low level of inputs, and the outer curve describes the output combinations associated with twice the inputs.

Why does the product transformation curve have a negative slope? Because in order to get more out of one output the farm must give up some of the other output. For example, a farm that emphasises wheat production will devote less of its resources to produce *bajra*. The outer curve lies twice as far from the origin as the inner curve, signifying that this firm's production process exhibits constant returns to scale in the production of both crops.

1.2.1.1 The Production Function for Foodgrain Crops

Consider a production of a wheat, *bajra* or *tur* farming household using family as well as hired labour, land suitable for growing these crops, fertilisers, seeds, irrigation like tube wells, bore wells and canals, credit facilities and expensive equipment like tractors. So production of these crops is a function of these inputs like equipment etc., which are fixed inputs in the short run.

1.2.1.2 Perfectly Competitive Market for these Products[2]

The market for these foodgrain crops is an example of an almost perfectly competitive market. Many farmers produce identical products, and transaction costs are negligible. Wheat is sold in a formal exchange or market such as a commodity exchange. Transaction costs are negligible. No time is wasted and transactions are instantaneous. Every buyer and seller in the market knows the market prices, quantities and qualities of wheat available at any moment.

The short run equilibrium for the agricultural market in our sample would be determined by the equilibrium of the market supply curve as defined below and the market demand curve.[3]

1.2.1.3 The Competitive Farmer's Short-run Supply Curve

The relevance of this concept is to illustrate the microeconomic theory underlying the working of market production or supply for an individual (perfectly competitive) farmer operating in the economy, with given price obtainable for the product of the farmer and given costs of producing the output.

A supply curve for a farmer tells us how much output it will produce at every possible price. We know that competitive farmer will increase output to the point at which price is equal to marginal cost, but it will not produce for the market if price is below average variable cost. Therefore, the farmer's supply curve is the portion of the marginal cost curve for which the marginal cost is greater than the average variable cost.

2. Perloff, 2001: 224.
3. Ibid.

We can illustrate the short-run supply curve with a figure. Note that for any P greater than minimum AVC, the profit-maximising output can be read directly from the graph. At a price P1, for example, the quantity supplied will be q_1; and at P_2, it will be q_2. For P less than (or equal to) minimum AVC, the profit-maximising output is equal to zero. In the Figure the entire short-run supply curve consists of the crosshatched portion of the vertical axis plus the marginal cost curve above the point of minimum average variable cost.

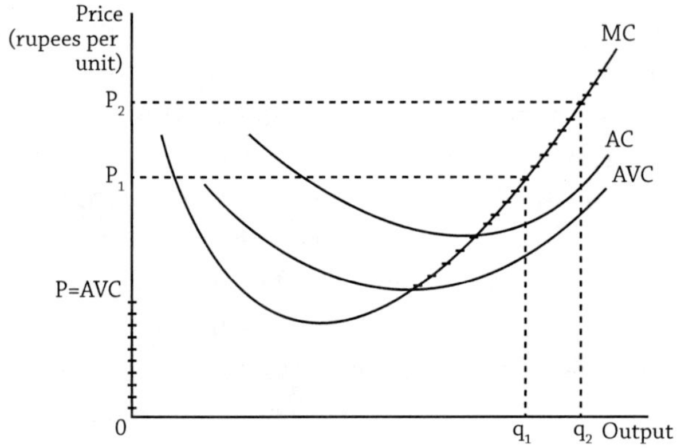

Short-run supply curves for competitive farms slope upward for the same reason that marginal cost increases-the presence of diminishing marginal returns to one or more factors of production. As a result, an increase in the market price will induce those farms already in the market to increase the quantities they produce. Higher price not only makes the additional production profitable, but also increases the firm's total profit because it applies to all the units that the farmer produces.

1.2.1.4 The Farmer's Response to an Input Price Change

When the price of product changes the farmer also changes its output level to ensure that the marginal cost of production remains equal to the price. Often, however the product price changes at the same time that the prices of inputs change. In this section, we show how the farmer's output decision changes in response to a change in the price of one of its inputs.

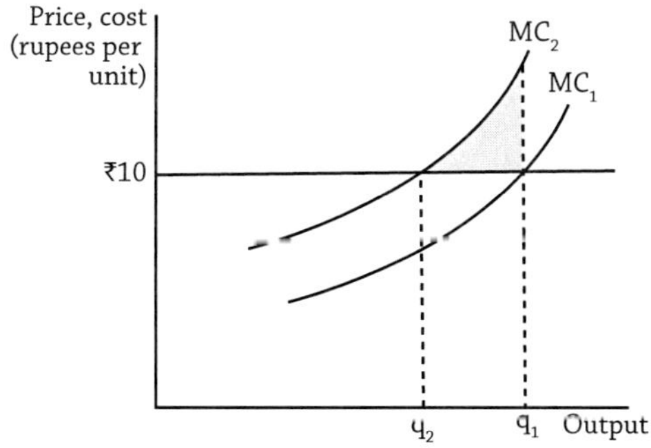

Figure shows a farm's marginal cost curve that is initially given by MC_1 when the farmer faces a price of ₹10 for its product. The farm maximises profit by producing an output of q_1. Now suppose the price of one input increases. Because it now costs more to produce each unit of output, this increase causes the marginal cost curve to shift upward from MC_1 to MC_2. The new profit-maximising output is q_2, at which $P= MC_2$. Thus, the higher input price causes the farm to reduce its output.

If the farm had continued to produce q_1, it would have incurred a loss on the last unit of production. In fact, all production beyond q_2 would reduce profit. The shaded area in the figure gives the total savings to the farm (or equivalently, the reduction in lost profit) associated with the reduction in output from q_1 to q_2.

1.2.1.5 The Short–run Market (Aggregate) Supply Curve

The short-run market (for say, wheat) supply curve shows the amount of (wheat) output that the farmers will produce in the short-run for every possible price. The market output is the sum of the quantities supplied by all of the individual farmers. Therefore, the market supply curve can be obtained by adding the supply curves of each of these farms. Figure shows how this is done when there are only three farmers, all of which have different short-run production costs. Each farmer's marginal cost curve is drawn only for the portion that lies above its average variable cost curve. (We have only shown three farmers to keep the graph simple, but the same analysis applies when there are many farms.)

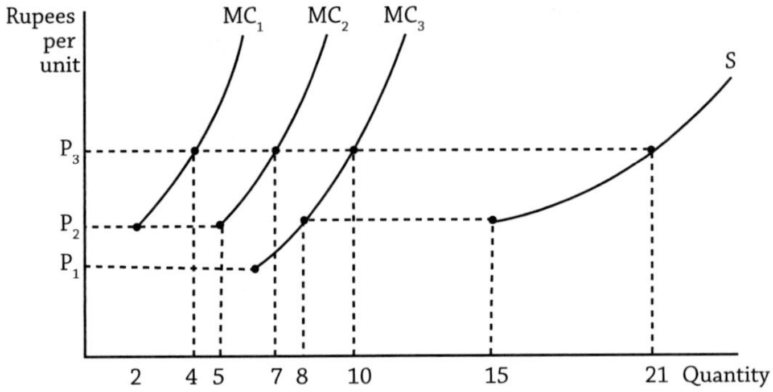

At any price below P_1, the farmers will produce no marketable output because P_1 is the minimum average variable cost of the lowest cost farm. Between P_1 and P_2, only farm 3 will produce. The wheat supply curve, therefore, will be identical to that portion of farmer 3's marginal cost curve MC_3. At price P_2, the market wheat supply will be the sum of the quantity supplied by all three farms. Farm 1 supply 2 units, farm 2 supplies 5 units, and farm 3 supplies 8 units. Aggregate supply is thus 15 units. At price P_3, farm 1 supplies 4 units, farm 2 supplies 7 units, and farm 3 supplies 10 units; the aggregate market supply is 21 units. Note that the market supply curve is upward sloping but has a kink at price P_2, the lowest price at which all three farms produce. With many farms in the market, however the kink becomes unimportant. Thus, we usually draw market supply as a smooth, upward-sloping curve.

1.2.1.6 Elasticity of Market Supply

Unfortunately, finding the aggregate supply curve is not always as simple as adding up a set of individual supply curves. As price rises, all wheat farms expand their output. This additional output increases the demand for inputs to production and may lead to higher input prices. As we saw above, increasing input prices shift a farmer's marginal cost curve upward. For example, an increased demand for milk could also increase demand for cow feed (which is used to feed cattle) and thereby cause its prices to rise. In turn, higher input prices will cause firms' marginal cost curves to shift upward. This increase lowers each farm's output choice (for any given market price) and causes the wheat market supply curve to be less responsive to changes in output price than it otherwise would be.

The price elasticity of market supply measures the sensitivity of (wheat) output to market price. The elasticity of supply Es is the percentage change in quantity supplied Q in response to a 1-per cent change in price P.

$E_s = (\Delta Q/Q) / (\Lambda P/P)$

Since marginal cost curves are upward sloping, the short run elasticity of supply is always positive. When marginal cost increases rapidly in response to increases in output, the elasticity of supply is low. In the short run, farms are capacity constrained and find it costly to increase output. But when marginal cost increases slowly in respond to increases in output, supply is relatively elastic; in this case, a small price increase induces farms to produce more.

1.2.1.7 The Effects of Increase in Cost of Output (or any such change) on Farm's Output[4]

Consider ways in which a farm responds to an increase in cost of its output. To simplify this analysis, assume that the firm uses a fixed-proportions production technology.

First, suppose the increase in cost (because of say, a pest attack leading to higher use of pesticide) affects only this farm and thus does not affect the market price of the product. We will see that the increase in cost of output encourages the farm to reduce its output. Figure shows the relevant short-run cost curves for a farm enjoying positive economic profit by producing an output of q_1 and selling its product at the market price P_1. This raises the marginal cost from MC_1 to MC_2. This also raises the average variable cost curve.

The increase in costs can have two possible effects. If the farm can still earn a positive or zero economic profit after the increase in costs, it will maximise its profit by choosing an output level at which increased marginal cost is equal to the price of the product. Its output falls from q_1 to q_2, and the supply curve shifts upward (by the amount

4. Ibid.: 251-52.

of the cost increase). If the firm can no longer earn an economic profit after the increase in marginal cost, it will choose to exit the market.

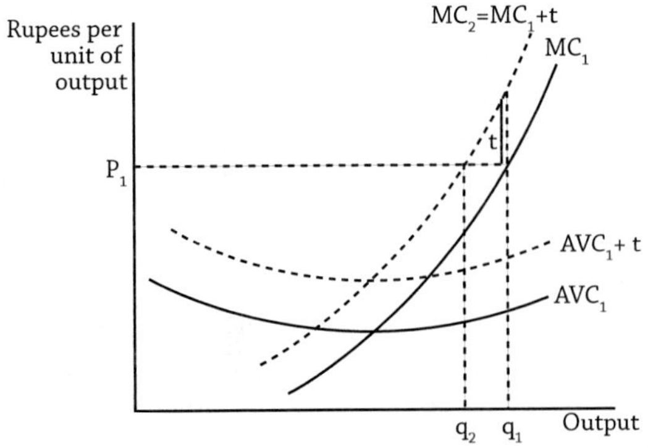

Now suppose that this pest attack influences every wheat farm in the region and so has increasing marginal costs. Because each farm reduces its output at the current market price, the total output supplied by the wheat farms in the region will also fall, causing the price of the product to increase. Figure illustrates this. An upward shift in the supply curve from S_1 to S_2, causes the market price of the product to increase from P_1 to P_2. Note that this increase is less than the cost increase. The increase in pr in price diminishes some of the effects we described previously. Farms will reduce the output less than they would without a price increase.

Finally, such effects may encourage some farmers (those whose costs are somewhat higher than others) to exit the wheat market. This raises the long-run average cost for each wheat farm.

1.2.1.8 Price Supports and Production Quotas[5]

Besides imposing a minimum price, the government can increase the price of a good in other ways. Much of Indian agricultural policy is based on a system of price-supports, whereby the government sets the market price of a good above the free-market level and buys up whatever output is needed to maintain that price. The government can also increase price by restricting production, either directly or through

5. Ibid.: 271-79.

incentives to producers. In this section, we show how these policies work and examine their impact on consumers, producers and the state budget.

1.2.1.9 Price Supports

In India, price supports aim to increase the prices of rice, wheat, jute, cotton, sugarcane and so on, so that the producers of those goods can receive higher incomes. Under a price support programme, the government sets a support price P_s and then buys up whatever output is needed to keep the market price at this level. Figure illustrates this. Let us examine the resulting losses to consumers, producers and the government

1.2.1.10 Consumers

At price P_s, the quantity that consumers demand falls to Q_1, but the quantity supplied increases to Q_2. To maintain this price and avoid having inventories pile up in producer warehouses, the government must buy the quantity $Qg= Q_2- Q_1$. In effect, because the government adds its demand Qg to the demand of consumers, producers can sell all they want at price P_s.

Because those consumers who purchase the good must pay a higher price P_s, instead of P_o, they suffer a loss of consumer surplus given by rectangle A. Because of the higher price, other consumers no longer buy the good or buy less of it, and their loss of surplus is given by triangle B. So, as with the minimum price that we examined above, consumers lose, in this case by an amount of $\Delta CS = -A-B$.

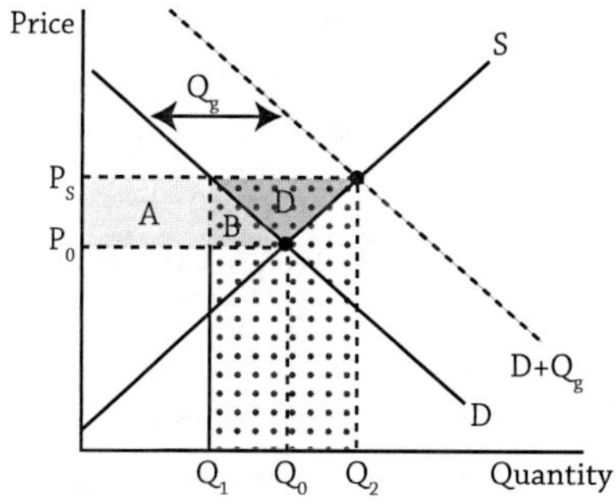

1.2.1.11 Producers

Producers gain (which is why such a policy is implemented). Producers are now selling a larger quantity Q_2 instead of Q_0, and at a higher price P_s. Observe from the figure that producer surplus increases by the amount $\Delta PS = A+B+D$.

1.2.1.12 Government

But there is also a cost to the government (which must be paid for by taxes, and so is ultimately a cost to consumers). That cost is $(Q_2-Q_1)P_s$, which is what the government must pay for the amount it purchases. In Figure this amount is represented by the large specked rectangle. This cost may be reduced if the government can 'dump' some of its purchases, i.e., sell them abroad at a low price. Doing so however, hurts the ability of domestic producers to sell in foreign markets, and it is domestic producers that the government is trying to please in the first place.

What is the total welfare cost of this policy? To find out, we add the change in consumer surplus to the change in producer surplus and then subtract the cost to the government. Thus, the total change in welfare is $\Delta CS + \Delta PS$ - Cost to Govt.=D-$(Q_2-Q_1)P_s$.

In terms of Figure, society as a whole is worse off by an amount given by the large specked rectangle, less triangle D.

This welfare loss can be very large. But the most unfortunate part of this policy is the fact that there is a much more efficient way to help farmers. If the objective is to give farmers an additional income equal to A+B+D, it is far less costly to society to give this money directly rather than *via* price supports. Because price supports are costing consumers A+B anyway, by paying farmers directly, society saves the large speckled rectangle, less triangle D. So why doesn't the government simply give farmers money? Perhaps because price supports are a less obvious give away and therefore politically more attractive.

1.2.1.13 Production Quotas

Besides entering the market and buying up output—thereby increasing total demand—the government can also cause the price of a good to rise by reducing supply. It can do this by decree—that is, by simply setting quotas on how much each farmer can produce. With appropriate quotas, the price can then be forced up to any arbitrary level.

This is exactly how many city governments maintain high taxi fares. They limit total supply by requiring each taxicab to procure a licence to ply on city's roads, and then limit the total number of licences. Another example is the control of liquor licences by state governments. By requiring any bar or restaurant that serves alcohol to have a liquor licence and then limiting the number of licences, entry by new restaurateurs is limited, which allows those who have licences to earn higher prices and profit margins.

The welfare effects of production quotas are shown in the figure. The government restricts the quantity supplied to Q_1, rather than the market-clearing level Q_0. Thus, the supply curve becomes the vertical line *S'* at Q_1. Consumer surplus is reduced by rectangle A (those consumers who buy the good pay a higher price) plus triangle B (at this higher price, some consumers no longer purchase the good). Producers gain rectangle A (by selling at a higher price) but lose triangle C (because they now produce and sell Q_1 rather than Q_0). Once again, there is a deadweight loss, given by triangles B and C.

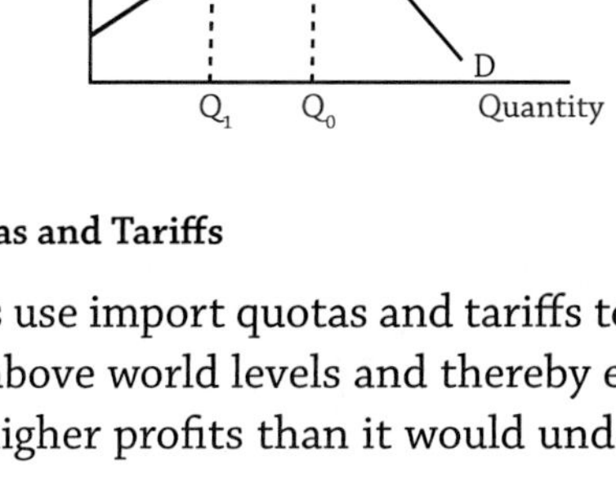

1.2.1.14 Import Quotas and Tariffs

Many countries use import quotas and tariffs to keep the domestic price of a product above world levels and thereby enable the domestic industry to enjoy higher profits than it would under free trade. As we will see, the cost to taxpayers from this protection can be high, with the loss to consumers exceeding the gain to domestic producers.

Without a quota or tariff, a country will import a good when its world price is below the price that would prevail domestically were there no imports. Figure illustrates this principle. S and D are the domestic demand and supply curves. If there were no imports, the domestic price and quantity would be P_o and Q_o, which equate demand and supply. But because the world price P_w is below P_o, domestic consumers have an incentive to purchase from abroad and will do so if imports are not restricted. How much will be imported? The domestic price will fall to the world price P_w; at this lower price, domestic production will fall to Q_s, and domestic consumption will rise to Q_d. Imports are then the difference between domestic consumption and domestic production, Q_d-Q_s.

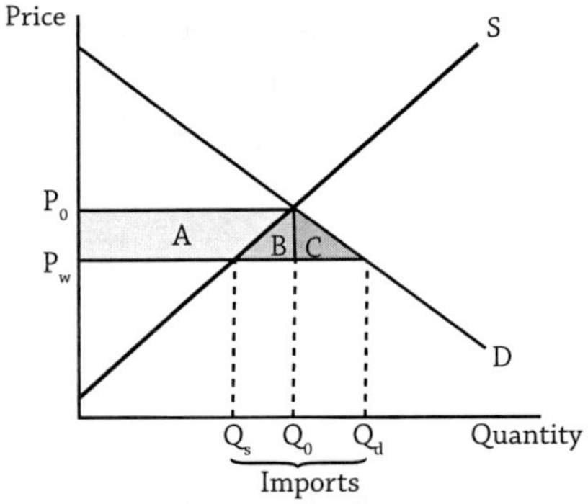

Now suppose the government, bowing to pressure from the domestic industry, eliminates imports by imposing a quota of zero-that is forbidding any importation of the good. What are the gains and losses of such a policy?

With no imports allowed, the domestic price will rise to Po. Consumers who still purchase the good (in quantity Qo) will pay more and will lose an amount of surplus given by trapezoid A and triangle B. In addition, given this higher price, some consumers will no longer buy the good, so there is an additional loss of consumer surplus, given by triangle C. The total change in consumer surplus is therefore $\Delta CS = -A-B-C$.

What about producers? Output is now higher (Q_o instead of Q_s) and is sold at a higher price (P_o instead of P_w). Producer surplus therefore increases by the amount n of trapezoid A: $\Delta PS = A$.

The change in total surplus $\Delta CS + \Delta PS$, is therefore $-B-C$. Again, there is a deadweight loss; consumers lose more than producers gain.

Imports could also be reduced to zero by imposing a sufficiently large tariff. The tariff would have to be equal to or greater than the difference between P_o and P_w. With a tariff of this size, there will be no imports, and therefore no government revenue from tariff collections, so the effect on consumers and producers would be the same as with a quota.

1.2.1.15 Market Supply of Inputs

The market supply curve for a factor input is usually upward sloping. We know that the market supply for a good sold in a competitive market is usually upward sloping because the marginal cost of producing the good is typically increasing. This is also the case for agricultural and other raw material inputs.

When the input is labour, however, people rather than firms are making supply decisions. In this case, utility maximisation by workers rather than profit maximisation by firms determine supply. In the discussion that follows, we use the analysis of income and substitution effects to show that although the market supply curve for labour can be upward sloping, it may also be, as in Figure, backward bending. In other words, a higher wage rate can lead to less labour being supplied

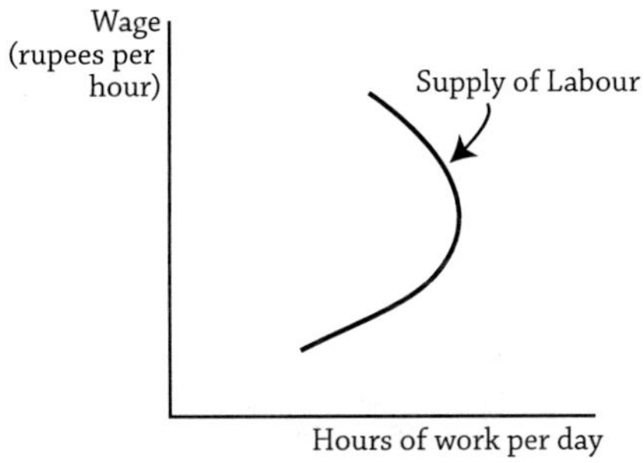

To see why a labour supply curve may be backward bending, divide the day into hours of work and hours of leisure. *Leisure* is a term that

describes enjoyable non-work activities, including sleeping and eating. *Work* benefits the worker only through the income it generates. We also assume that a worker has the flexibility to choose how many hours per day to work.

The wage rate measures the price that the farm labourer places on leisure time, because his or her wage measures the amount of money the worker gives up to enjoy leisure. As the wage rate increases, therefore, the price of leisure also increases. This price change brings about a substitution effect (a change in relative price with utility held constant) and an income effect (a change in utility with relative prices unchanged). There is a substitution effect because the higher price of leisure encourages workers to substitute work for leisure. An income effect occurs because the higher wage rate increases the worker's purchasing power. With higher income, the worker can buy more of many goods, one of which is leisure. If more leisure was chosen, it is because the income effect has encouraged the worker to work fewer hours. Income effects can be large because wages are the primary component of most people's income. When the income effect outweighs the substitution effect the result is a backward bending supply curve.

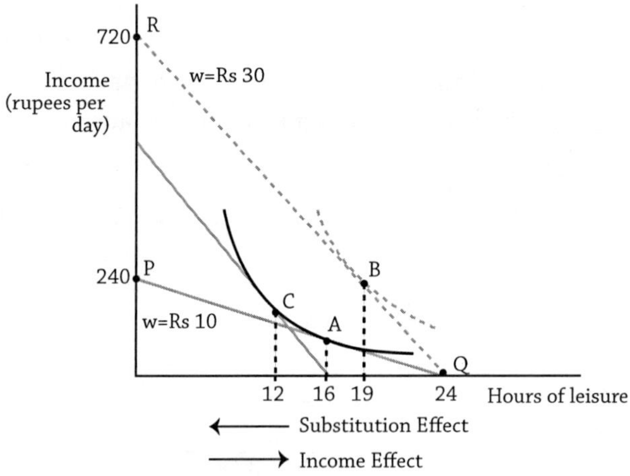

Figure illustrates how a backward-bending supply curve for labour can result from the work-leisure decision for a typical weekday. The horizontal axis shows hours of leisure per day, the vertical axis income generated by work. (We assume there are no other sources of income.) Initially the wage rate is ₹10 per hour, and the budget line is given by PQ. Pont P, for example, shows that if an individual worked a 24-hour day he would earn an income of ₹240.

The worker maximises utility by choosing point A, thus enjoying 16 hours of leisure per day (with 8 hours of work) and earning ₹80. When the wage rate increases to ₹30 per hour, the budget line rotates about the horizontal intercept to line RQ. (Only 24 hours of leisure are possible.) Now the worker maximises utility at B by choosing 19 hours of leisure per day (with 5 hours of work), while earning ₹150. If only the substitution effect came into play, the higher wage rate would encourage the worker to work 12 hours (at C) instead of 8. However, the income effect works in the opposite direction. It overcomes the substitution effect and lowers the work day from 8 hours to 5.

In real life, a backward bending labour supply curve might apply to a farm labourer working during the summer season to earn money for expenses. As soon as a target level of earnings is reached, the labourer stops working and allocates more time to leisure. An increase in the wage rate will then lead to fewer hours worked because it enables the labourer to reach the target level of earnings more quickly.

1.2.2 General Equilibrium Analysis[6]

So far we have used a partial-equilibrium analysis: an examination of equilibrium and changes in equilibrium in one market in isolation. However in our study we not only have multiple crop products and multiple inputs but the marketed surplus function which relates to the production, retention and distress sales in the different crops. We have briefly covered the theory of such an interrelated analysis in our discussion of agricultural household.

1.2.2.1 Efficiency in Exchange

Economic efficiency or Pareto efficiency arises when, no one can be made better off without making someone else worse off.

6. Perloff, 2001: 306

1.2.2.2 The Advantages of Trade

Whenever two consumers MRS's are different there is scope for Trade. To achieve economic efficiency MRS must be equal. Consider, the following Table:

Individual	*Initial Allocation*	*Trade*	*Final Allocation*
Rajan	7F,1C	-1F,+1C	6F,2C
Maya	3F,5C	+1F,-1C	4F,4C

Now, even if trade from an inefficient allocation makes both people better off, the new allocation is not necessarily efficient.

When the indifference curves are tangent, one person cannot be made better off without making the other person worse off. That is an efficient allocation.

If Rajan is an effective bargainers, trade might change the allocation of goods, to where Maya is no worse off and Rajan is much better off.

The Contract Curve

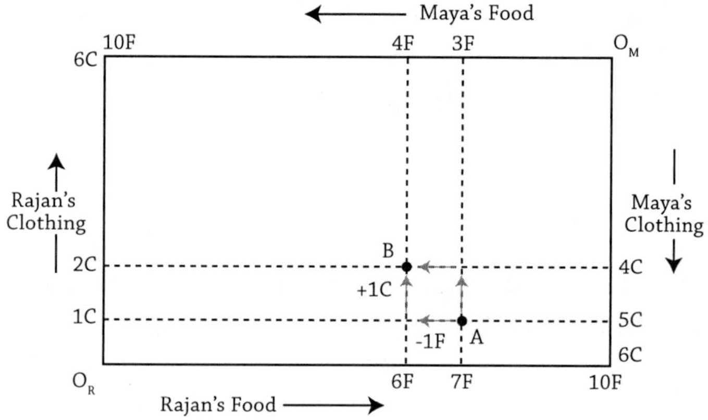

To find all possible efficient allocations of food and clothing between Maya and Rajan, we look for all points of tangency between each of their indifference curves.

These allocations are efficient because there is no way to reallocate goods to make someone better off without making someone else worse off.

Once a point on a contract curve, has been chosen, there is no way to move to another point on the contract curve without making one person worse off.

We can frequently improve efficiency even when one aspect of a proposed change makes someone worse off. We need only include a second change, such that the combined set of changes leaves someone better off and no one worse off.

1.2.2.3 Consumer Equilibrium in a Competitive Market

We can show how competitive markets lead to efficient exchange by using the Edgeworth Box Diagram to mimic a competitive market. Suppose for example there are many Rajans and many Mayas.

Figure shows the opportunities for trade when we start at the allocation given by point A and when the price of both food and clothing are equal to 1. When the prices of food and clothing are equal, each unit of food can be exchanged for 1 unit of clothing.

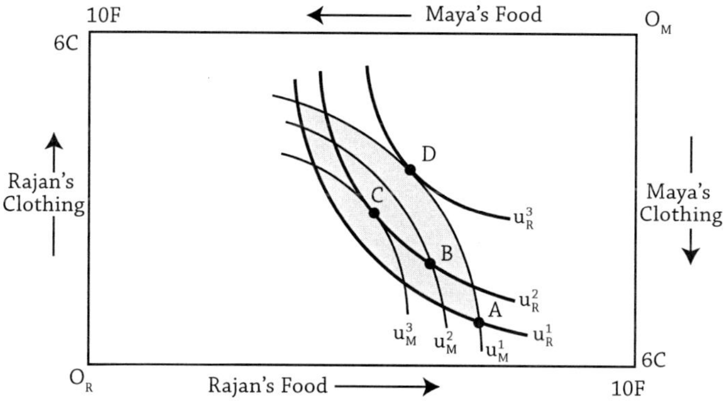

Suppose each Rajan decides to buy 2 units of clothing and sell 2 units of food in exchange. This would move each Rajan from A to C. Meanwhile, each Maya buys 2 units of food and sells 2 units of clothing. This would move each Maya from A to C as well.

An quilibrium is a set of prices at which the quantity demanded equals the quantity supplied in every market. This is also a competitive equilibrium because all suppliers and demanders are price takers.

In a competitive market, prices will adjust if there is excess demand in some markets(the quantity demanded of one good is greater than the quantity supplied) and excess supply in others (the quantity supplied is greater than the quantity demanded.)

1.2.2.4 The Economic Efficiency of Competitive Markets

- We can see from point C in figure that the allocation in a competitive equilibrium is economically efficient.
- IC's are tangent so MRS between consumers is equal.
- Each IC is tangent to price line, so MRS is equal to ratio of prices.
- Minimum of information is required. Their preferences and prices they face must be known by consumers, but not what is produced or demands of other consumers.

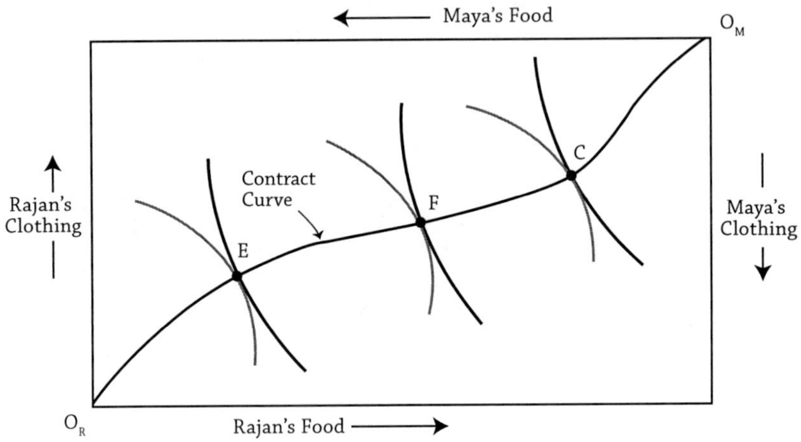

1.3 Agricultural Household Models

A Theoretical Framework Related to Agricultural Market[7]

To set the stage further, an agricultural market is studied very well with the help of agricultural household models. Most households in agricultural areas produce partly for sale and partly for own consumption. They also purchase some of their inputs such as fertiliser and labour and provide some inputs such as family labour from their own resources. Any change in the policies governing agricultural activities will therefore affect not only production but

7. Singh (1986.)

also consumption and labour supply. Agricultural household models are designed to capture these interactions in a theoretically consistent fashion; this process is very illustrative for marketed surplus.

For example suppose we examine the effects of alternative policies on the well-being of representative agricultural households. Well-being may be interpreted here to mean household income or some other measure such as nutritional status. For example, in examining the effect of a policy designed to provide cheap food for urban consumers, an agricultural household model would allow the analyst to assess the costs to farmers of depressed producer prices. The nutritional benefits for the urban population may be more than offset by the reduced nutritional status of the rural population that results from lower farm incomes. In this way the simultaneous effect of incomes and purchases i.e. production and consumption both of which are relevant for estimating marketed surplus come into existence. Second, an understanding of the behaviour of agricultural households would shed light on the spill over effects of government policies on other segments of the rural population. For example, since most investment strategies are designed to increase production, their primary impact is on the incomes of agricultural households. As a result, rural investment strategies may not reach landless households or households engaged in non-agricultural activities. A model that incorporates total labour demand and family labour supply, however, would allow the analyst to explore the effects of investment policy on the demand for hired labour and hence on the rural labour market and the incomes of landless households. We already know that for estimating marketed surplus the payment to hired labour is an important element.

Similarly, a model that incorporates consumer behaviour would allow the analyst to explore the consequences of increased profits for agricultural households on the demand for products and services provided by non-agricultural, rural households. Since the demand for non-agricultural commodities is often thought to be much more responsive to an increase in income than the demand for agricultural staples, this spill over effect may well be important. This estimation helps us determine the change in consumption of agricultural households which is an important element of marketed surplus.

Since agricultural household models capture both consumption and production behaviour, they are an appropriate vehicle for examining the effect of pricing policy on marketed surplus, the government is obliged to consider how agricultural households will alter their production and consumption in response to changes in prices.

This approach offers important policy insights that differ significantly from the results of more traditional approaches in which production and consumption decisions are examined separately. It is important to treat the main household decisions in a consistent manner for a policy relevant variable such as marketed surplus. To begin with let us explain the theoretical framework in which the entire model is specified. For any production cycle, the household is assumed to maximise a utility function: where the commodities are an agricultural staple, a market-purchased good, and leisure. Utility is maximised subject to a cash income constraint. The household also faces a time constraint; it cannot allocate more time to leisure, on-farm production, or off-farm employment than the total time available to the household. It also faces a production constraint or production technology that depicts the relationship between inputs and farm output. In this presentation, various complexities are omitted. For example, the possibility of more than one crop is ignored. In addition, it is assumed that family labour and hired labour are perfect substitutes and can be added directly. Production is also assumed to be riskless. Finally, and perhaps most importantly, it is assumed that the four prices in the model are not affected by actions of the household.

The three constraints on household behaviour can be collapsed into a single constraint; which includes a measure of farm profits. In this constraint on the left hand side we include total household "expenditure" on three items: the market-purchased commodity, the household's "purchase" of its own output, and the household's "purchase" of its own time in the form of leisure. The constraint on the right hand side includes Becker's concept of full income, in which the value of the stock of time owned by the household is explicitly recorded, as is any labour income. The extension for agricultural households is the inclusion of a measure of farm profits, with all labour valued at the market wage, this being a consequence of the assumption of price taking behaviour in the labour market. The utility function and the household constraint are the core of all the studies of agricultural households reported here. They reveal that the household can choose the levels of consumption for the three commodities, the total labour input, and the fertiliser input into agricultural production.

That is, having first maximised profits, the household then maximises utility subject to its (maximised) value of full income. This demonstrates, given the assumptions made about markets, that even though the household's production and consumption decisions may be simultaneous in time, they can be modelled recursively. The presence of farm profits in the constraint demonstrates the principal message of the farm household literature-that farm technology, quantities of fixed inputs, and prices of variable inputs and outputs affect consumption decisions. The positive effect of an increase in profits (and hence farm income), an effect totally ignored in traditional models of demand, will definitely dampen and may outweigh the negative effect of both income and substitution in standard consumer demand theory. The presence of the profit effect is a direct consequence of the joint treatment of production and consumption decisions.

1.4 The Concepts of Marketed and Marketable Surplus

Marketable surplus is a theoretical normative *ex ante* concept which represents the surplus which the farmer/producer has available with himself for disposal once the genuine requirements of the farmer's family consumption, payment of wages in kind, feed, seed and wastage have been met. Marketed surplus as compared to marketable surplus is a practical *ex-post* concept and refers to that part of the marketable surplus which is marketed by the producer i.e., not only the part which is available for disposal but that part which is made available to the market or to the disposal of the non-farm rural and urban population. The farmer, in case of commercial agriculture, is motivated by profit considerations, so he takes his whole produce to the market and purchases his requirement from the market, but in the case of subsistence agriculture, the concept of marketed and marketable surplus becomes relevant as the farmer generally produces for his own subsistence and it is only the remainder left after meeting his own requirements, that is taken to the market for sale. The concept of "marketable surplus" is subjective because the feature of retention of the farmer is a matter of subjective guess. The concept of "marketed surplus", on the other hand, is objective, because it refers specifically to the marketed amount i.e., to the actual quantity which enters the market.

In most cases, the marketed part may be less than the theoretically marketable part because out of the marketable part, the farmer may be willing to sell only a part. He may hoard part of it in anticipation of rising price of the grain or for some other reasons. In certain cases, marketed surplus may be greater than the marketable surplus. This happens when the farmers are driven to distress sales. There may be the case of a subsistence farmer who has produced just to meet his family consumption requirements. But he may take some portion of his produce to the market to meet his immediate cash obligations. In such cases, the marketed surplus released by the farmer will not be the real one also the portion marketed will be greater than what he considers marketable because of distress sales (Sadhu and Singh, 2000).

1.4.1 Computation of Marketable and Marketed Surplus

Marketable Surplus

It is computed by the formula

A – B = MS,

where MS is marketable surplus, A stands for net availability of the given crop in the year of reference and B stands for the following items in the same year:

1. consumption by the farm family;
2. consumption by permanent labour engaged on the farm;
3. consumption by the temporary labour occasionally employed on the farm;
4. quantity retained for seed;

5. quantity retained as feed for farm animals;
6. quantity retained for barter;
7. payments in kind:
   a. to permanent labour,
   b. to temporary labour,
   c. for machinery and equipment,
   d. for customary payments,
   e. to land owners as rent,
   f. to land owners as share of produce,
   g. for re-payment of loan,
   h. land revenue,
   i. irrigation charges, and
   j. others;
8. physical losses:
   a. in threshing and winnowing ,
   b. in transport from threshing floor to storage, and
   c. in storage at producer's level.

Consumption by the Farm Family

The term 'consumption by the farm family' of the cultivator households has two distinct connotations in so far as its impact on marketed and marketable surplus is concerned. For marketed surplus, it refers to the quantity actually retained for consumption by the family irrespective of the actual total requirements for the purpose. For marketable surplus it refers to the quantity that ought to be retained by the farm family for its consumption or the quantity required for consumption.

The marginal or small farmer produces something and plans to dispose off some amount in the market, but due to compulsions he is forced to sell off a certain amount just to meet his immediate cash requirements. For example, he may sell at low price during harvest time and buy back at lean period at high price. So in this case the quantity retained will be less than that planned to be retained and marketed surplus will be less than marketable.

The use of the term "surplus" would thus be justified only if the quantity actually required for consumption, rather than the quantity actually retained for consumption is taken into account for arriving at the quantity of marketable surplus actually available for non-farm consumption.

In case the quantity actually retained for consumption (and not the quantity actually required for consumption) is taken into account, the quantity calculated is the marketed surplus, that portion of production which actually enters the market, which is in this sense a net concept where from net availability we subtract sales including distress sales and also net our purchases and repurchases (Newman, 1977). In case of marketable surplus, instead of quantity retained for family consumption, the quantity required for consumption/planned (ought to be retained) is taken into consideration for calculation of marketable surplus and in this sense it is a gross concept with the required consumption concept not considering distress sales and repurchases. The quantity required for family consumption has been calculated by adding the 'quantity retained for family consumption + quantity purchased for family consumption + total receipts in kind for family consumption'.

The marketable surplus will thus be according to the formula:

$A - B = MS$,

where A stands for production and B includes all the items mentioned earlier except that 'quantity required for consumption' has been treated to include the quantity required for 'family consumption' as explained above and MS stands for 'marketable surplus'. This quantity is actually available for non-farm consumption and is, therefore, true marketable surplus.

Computation of Marketed Surplus

In case the quantity actually retained for consumption (and not the quantity actually required for consumption) is taken into account, the quantity calculated is the marketed surplus i.e., the quantity consumed (including buy-backs or repurchases) is netted out from net availability or production in time t plus minus change in stocks and the sales including distress sales are also netted out.

The marketed surplus will thus be according to the formula:

A – B = MS,

where A stands for production and B includes all the items mentioned earlier apart from 8 physical losses: c) in storage at producer's level. The term 'consumption by the farm family' of the cultivator households refers to the quantity actually retained for consumption by the family irrespective of the actual total requirements for the purpose.

For accounting purpose we have,

Marketable surplus = Production of the crop in the year –Retention including all seed, feed and wastage – Required consumption including purchases.

Marketed Surplus = Net availability of the crop in the year – Retention included seed, feed and wastage losses apart from losses at producer level – Actual consumption. The unforeseen changes such as distress sales, hoarding or repurchases which the farmer undertakes and thus changes his position vis-a-vis the market is taken into account ex post. Thus, the concept is a net one inclusive of these changes vis-a-vis the market (Newman, 1977). Therefore, dynamic exigencies are considered in marketed surplus.

Note the buyback or repurchases could be due to

1. Storage problems leading farmer to sell after harvest and buyback in the next year before harvest, note here the net sale and consumption remains the same but you just adjust the time of sale and purchase first selling and then buying.
2. Compelling circumstances at time of harvest and post harvest.
3. High seasonality in prices.
4. Unusual circumstances makes expectations go wrong.

Nowadays buy back is less seen what is seen is the farmer selling at harvest season at low price rather than selling at high price in lean season (inter temporal changes in sale period and amount)

1.4.2 Factors Influencing Marketable Surplus

The *Directorate of Marketing and Inspection Report of 2002* studies this issue more deeply. The quantum of marketable surplus is influenced by the factors operating both in the pre-production and post-production stages.

Pre-production Factors

The factors operating in the pre-production stages are those which determine the level of production i.e., physical area under the crop, investment of resources including inputs, productivity of the crop, expectations of monetary returns from the sale of crop, etc.

Post-production Factors

The post-production factors influencing marketable surplus are: physical demand for human and animal consumption on the farm, local customs and practices regarding cash and kind payments, socio-economic conditions of the producers, price policies and price realisation etc.

Infrastructural and Other Facilities

These influence production and marketable surplus and other entities in turn get reinforced or weakened by infrastructural and other facilities existing in the economy in general, and rural economy in particular. Some of these are:

i) Availability of Irrigation Facilities

It is very well known that irrigation facility influences the productivity coupled with other inputs.

ii) Connectivity by Roads

This is the most important facility for villages, particularly if these are connected by *pucca* all-weather roads. Absence of this connectivity becomes a handicap and a blockade in exchange between rural and urban sector. This influences the difficulties and cost of transportation, compelling sales in villages, restriction of flow of supplies to and demand from urban trade centres and increased uneconomic elements in price spread between the producers and the consumers. These drawbacks in turn lead to some of the basic pitfalls of the agricultural sector such as cropping pattern, less responsive forces of market, subsistence farming rather than market-oriented farming.

iii) Distance of a Village from the Market(s)

The distance between the village and a market is one of the determinants of the type of crops to be produced and marketed in different areas. As the distance from the village to the market increases, the village goes beyond market influence and the result is subsistence farming in such villages. A longer distance with good road and quick means of transport is fairly less serious drawback than short distance without proper roads and proper means of transport.

iv) Services of Regulated Market(s)

Regulated markets provide services for fair participation on the part of the buyers and sellers by eliminating imperfections and also by eliminating malpractices. Since the regulation of market is for the benefit of the farmers or producers, it has positive impact on production and the marketable surplus, in general.

v) Storage Facilities in Village(s)

Proper storage facilities are essentially a basic need to save the produce from the physical losses caused by improper sanitation and hygiene. Improper sanitation and hygiene is instrumental for deterioration of quality due to infection of fungus, moulds and physical losses due to infection of insects and pests like rodents. Proper storage is necessary to retain the farm surplus at the producers' level for disposal at a later stage of the season when supply and demand are better placed and to recall the surplus matching with the demand of the entire season. Thus this factor also contributes to the production pattern and the marketable surplus.

From this interesting listing we can isolate the following specific factors determining marketable surplus.

1.4.3 Factors Determining Marketed Surplus

Let us analyse the factors determining marketed surplus. Srinivasan (1961) in a penetrating analysis based on his experience as a Director of the Department of Marketing and Inspection of the Ministry of Agriculture lays this issue bare. Dated, it is relevant even now.

> Thus it is seen that a multitude of factors act and interact on each other in the determination of marketed surpluses of food grains and commercial crops throughout the country. The vagaries of weather and the usual uncertain ties and hazards associated with agriculture are accentuated

> by man-made measures and psychological inhibitions, customs, usages and practices without even a rationale. These add to the difficulties confronting those who have to estimate the market arrivals of crops and the marketed surpluses of the same and the retention by the producers. It is extremely difficult in working out this equation to allow for the interference of so many factors.

He has an interesting classification of factors on which marketed surplus depends. These are:

1. Whether the crops in question are food crops or industrial crops?
2. The greatest single factor in the determination of marketed surplus is the retention for personal and family consumption.
3. Feeding of permanent and casual labourer—payment in kind for certain operations as harvesting.
4. Crop retained for feed of livestock.
5. Retention for seed—dependent on variety to be sown, area sown under particular crop and method of sowing. Local conditions and whether the crop is sown pure or mixed with other crops.
6. Standard of living—coarse grains or cereals, customs-dietary patterns, change in food habits, price and substitution.
7. Transport facilities—role in marketing of a crop.
8. Monetisation.
9. Size of holding, marketed surplus increases with size.
10. Price consciousness combined with capacity to withhold produce; off farm income.
11. Production of other crops including cereals.
12. Need for cash by producers, including access to cooperative credit.
13. Production for domestic use or for sale.
14. Availability of marketing facilities.
15. Total quantity produced.
16. Substitution due to rise in income, or rise in prices.
17. Role of government policies.
18. Practice of cultivators.

19. Financial position of producers.
20. Condition of storage.

1.5 Marketed Surplus and Marketable Surplus Concept: A Brief Literature Review[8]

1.5.1 Relationship between Marketed Surplus and Marketable Surplus

- Marketed surplus is more than marketable surplus when the farmer retains a smaller quantity of the crop than the actual requirements for family and farm needs. It is specially true for small and marginal farmers whose need for cash is immediate (distress sales).
- In case of large farmers having better retention capacity or in case of fall in relative price to a competing crop leading to substitution there is retention of the crop and marketed surplus may be less than the marketable surplus.
- In case of perishable commodities and for the average farmer, marketed surplus is equal to the marketable surplus (Acharya and Agarwal, 2010).

1.5.2 Relationship between Prices and Marketable Surplus

Two main hypotheses have been advanced to explain the relationship between prices and the marketable surplus of food grains.

1. *Inverse Relationship:* Mathur and Ezekiel (1961) postulate that the farmer's cash requirements are nearly fixed, and given the price level, the marketed portion of the output is determined. This implies that the farmers' consumption is a residual; this also implies that given a certain price, the marketed surplus and marketable surplus will vary inversely with the price level. This behaviour assumes that farmers have inelastic cash requirements. So the given cash requirements are to be satisfied from the marketed surplus, which will decrease when the price will rise and increase when the price will fall.

---

8. In this section, italics have been added in the text and quotes at various places by the author to emphasise the context of the approach to marketed surplus, i.e., which factor is being emphasised—size-class, state of development etc.

The argument is that, in the poor economy of underdeveloped countries, farmers sell that amount of the output which gives them the amount of money they need to satisfy their cash requirements; they retain the balance of output for their own consumption purposes. With a rise in the prices of food grains, they sell a smaller quantity of food grains to get the cash they need and *vice versa*. In other words, with a rise in price, farmers sell a smaller and with the fall in price, they sell a larger quantity. It has been argued (Krishnan, 1965) that the marketed surplus varies inversely with the market price. It is contended that a higher price for a subsistence crop may increase the producer's real income sufficiently to ensure that the income effect on demand for the consumption of the crop outweighs the price effect on production and consumption. Therefore, in fact, there is more real income with the farmer to consume the crop as compared to the higher price leading to greater production.

2. *Positive Relationship:* Krishna (1962; 1967) put forward the case for a positive relationship between prices and the marketed surplus of food grains in India. This relation is based on the assumption that farmers are price conscious. By farmers being more price conscious what will happen is that as prices will rise, farmers will sell more and retain less. As a result there is increased surplus. The converse, too, holds true. Raj Krishna has pointed that the elasticity of the marketable surplus is not negative so long as the substitution effect is non-zero. That is, when the price rises, the consumer prefers competitive crop and so marketable surplus increases.

Three models to indirectly investigate the size and magnitude of the elasticity of the marketed surplus of a subsistence crop are given below.

a) Krishna model:

$$M = Q - C$$

$$E = rb - (r-1)(g + mkh)$$

where

M = Marketed surplus of the crop,

Q = Total production of the crop,

C = On farm consumption of the crop,

r = Reciprocal of sales ratio (Q/M),

b = Output price elasticity of the crop,

g = Consumption price elasticity of the crop,

m = Sales ratio (M/Q),

h = Consumption income elasticity,

k = PQ/L=Ratio of the total value of production to the total net income of the producers.

b) Behrman model (1966):

$$M_1 = Q_1 - C_1$$

$$E = rb_1-(r-1)[q+kh(1+b_1)]-(r-1)hb_2(1-k)$$

where

M_1 = Marketed surplus of Q_1,

b_1 = Price elasticity of Q_1 with respect to P_1/P_2,

b_2 = Price elasticity of Q_2 with respect to P_1/P_2 and all other notations having the same meaning as defined earlier.

c) Krishnan model (1965):

$$E_m = -(\beta - \alpha)\, r/1 - r \quad 0<r<1$$

where,

R = Proportion of output consumed on farm,

β = Consumption income elasticity,

α = Consumption price elasticity.

d) Krishna Raj (1962): Krishna starts by defining market supply as:

$$M = Q-C$$

where

M was marketed surplus of a crop,

Q is its output, and

C is its consumption by the household.

If P denoted relative price and I the income of the farmer, then the expression was differentiated with respect to price

$$\partial M / \partial P = \partial Q / \partial P - \partial C / \partial P - \partial C / \partial I * \partial I / \partial P$$

If the peasant were only a producer of the crop of concern, the increase in income due to an increase in the price of the crop would be equal to the number of units of this crop which he produced. If the peasant were only a consumer of this crop, the decrease in income would be equal to number of units he consumed. Therefore, since he is both a producer and consumer:

$\partial I / \partial P = Q - C = M$

Substituting this equation into the previous equation results in:

$\partial M / \partial P = \partial Q / \partial P - \partial C / \partial P - M * \partial C / \partial I \; I$

Rearranging the terms and multiplying by P/M we get

P/M*

$\partial M / \partial P = Q / M * P / Q * \partial Q / \partial P - (Q / M - 1)$

$(P / C * \partial C / \partial P + M / Q * PQ / I * I) / C * \partial C / \partial I$

e = rb-(r-1)(g+mkh)

The result that Krishna obtains is: other things being equal, the elasticity of market supply varies inversely as the income elasticity of home consumption and the proportion of revenue from the crop to total income and inversely as the elasticity of total output and the absolute elasticity of substitution effect on home consumption.

Knowing the direction in which e is moved by the movement of each of the parameters, b, g, k and h, the author found it possible to estimate the lower and upper limits of e by choosing two sets of values of these parameters such that they gave us these limits. An important element of the authors calculations was that e is never negative so long as the substitution effect is non-zero. If b is positive, albeit small, the likelihood of a perverse market supply behaviour is extremely small.

The depletion of the market supplies of food crops due to crop failures is often misinterpreted as a reflection of a backward sloping market supply function. Thus if supply goes down because weather is bad, it is perceived that the farmer's behaviour is perverse. Krishna's analysis was a warning against such misinterpretations (Acharya and Agarwal, 2010).

1.5.3 Price Elasticity of the Marketed Surplus of a Subsistence Crop

Behrman (1966) is concerned primarily with the price response of the marketed surplus of a single crop for various adjustment periods. A model is derived for the estimation of this response. The derivation of the one previous model, which was formulated by Krishna, is examined. The implications of the two models for Punjabi wheat are contrasted. Finally, the model derived by Behrman is used to provide rough estimates of the price elasticity of the marketed surplus of Thai rice.

Krishnan (1965) examines the prevalent notion of inverse relationship between price and marketable surplus. He based his analysis on Mathur and Ezekiel (1961).

The crux of the matter is that in the short run, the total supply of food grains is fixed. Assuming that for near-subsistence farmers the cash requirements are fixed and therefore an inverse relationship may be postulated, why should a similar assumption be made for farmers above the subsistence level? To escape from this impasse, they further assume that farmers save in kind rather than money.

An algebraic expression for the elasticity of marketable surplus is derived by Krishnan (1965)

Let

$\bar{Q}$ = total output of food grains given in the short run (net of seed requirements etc.

P = price of food grains

$Y_a = \bar{Q}P$ = income of farmers

R = proportion of output consumed by the farmers themselves

$M = \bar{Q}$ (1-r)=marketable surplus

$r\bar{Q} = F(P, \bar{Q}P)$

Let the specific form of the demand function be of the constant elasticity type.

Then,

$r\bar{Q} = AP^{-\alpha} (\bar{Q}P)^{\beta}$

$= A \bar{Q}\ \beta\ p\ \beta - \alpha$

$R = A\ P\ \beta - \alpha\ \bar{Q}\ \beta - 1$

$M = 1\text{-}r)\ \bar{Q} = \bar{Q} - AP\ \beta - \alpha\ \bar{Q}\ \beta$

Differentiating this equation with respect to P, we obtain

$\partial M/ \partial P = -A\bar{Q}\,\beta\ p\ \beta{-}\alpha{-}1_{(\beta-\alpha)}$

The elasticity is given by

$\partial M / \partial P^{*}\ P/M = -A\bar{Q}\ \ \beta\ p\ \beta{-}\alpha{-}1_{(\beta-\alpha)} *\ P/\bar{Q}\ \text{-}A\bar{Q}\ \ \beta\ p\ \beta{-}\alpha$

$= -\ (\beta{-}\alpha)A\bar{Q}\ \ \beta\ p\ \beta{-}\alpha/\bar{Q} - A\bar{Q}\ \ \beta\ p\ \beta{-}\alpha$

This can be rewritten as

$E_M = -(\beta - \alpha)r/1-r$

In the above expression β and α are the income and price elasticity's of the farmers demand function and r is the proportion of output consumed by them.

If the price elasticity of demand is greater than the income elasticity, then the marketable surplus curve will have a positive slope. On the other hand, if the income elasticity exceeds the former, the whole expression will be negative and the marketable surplus will have a negative slope. In the latter case when the price rises, the income effect outweighs the substitution effect and therefore, own consumption increases.

The short-run nature of the phenomenon has been neglected sometimes by introducing an elasticity of supply with respect to price also into the equations. In that situation, the elasticity of the marketable surplus may become positive, if the supply elasticity outweighs the elasticity of consumption. That is, if more is produced there will be more marketed surplus. Krishna (1962), for instance, introduces the elasticity of supply into the expression. Krishna also assumes a demand function for the farmer in which bulk of his income does not enter at all. He assumes that farmers, consumption is a function of price and income from the sales of the marketable surplus only. In the notation of Krishnan, his demand function is as follows:

$D = F(P, P(1-r)Q)$.

Given a positive elasticity of supply and a demand function with the above variables, it is no wonder he concludes that the elasticity of marketable surplus "is never negative so long as the substitution effect is non-zero".

Bardhan (1970) concludes about marketed surplus with regard to state of development of farmers that:

> At the present stage the agricultural sector as a whole in countries like India may not necessarily market more grains during a year when grain price is going up, but this might be less evident for relatively more prosperous regions or farmers.

And further:

> Our results do show that the price elasticity of marketed surplus in the short run may be negative and since this forms a part of the long-run price elasticity the value of the latter, even when positive, will be lower than otherwise. Our results also seem to indicate that the poorer is the set of cultivators considered the more important is this possibility.

Bardhan and Bardhan (1971) construct a time series for marketed surplus of *cereals* for India as a whole. The elasticity of marketed proportion of cereals output with respect to price of cereals relative to manufactured consumables bought by the agricultural population is positive and has a value of near unity. The elasticity with respect to price of commercial crops relative to cereals is negative and has an absolute value significantly below unity. The elasticity with respect to the technological progress parameter is negative and has an absolute value that is significantly above unity.

Chand (1991) finds that the marketed surplus of *wheat* (italics mine) in Punjab showed great responsiveness to prices compared to its output supply. For *commercial crops*, the output supply and marketed surplus did not differ significantly from each other. Notwithstanding the low effect of producer and factor prices on output and market supply, their impact on net income of farmers was amazing.

Chattopadhyay and Sen (1988), came to the conclusion that the marketable surplus of any *subsistence crop* depends on the availability of cultivated land under the crop. Besides this, among the factors that permit the farmer to increase his marketable surplus, the most important one is his *family size.* If the family size is big, the marketable surplus will be relatively lower, even for the big-sized farms. Per capita availability of cultivated land among the larger farms is certainly higher compared to the smaller ones, but per capita availability of land under a specific crop need not be higher in the larger *size* groups than the smaller farms. The phenomenon of marketable surplus should be examined not in terms of *size-classes* of holdings but with the acreage of individual crops separately against each size-class.

Dubey (1963) argues that proportion of agricultural production that is marketed by the peasant has been assigned a significant role in some recent analyses of problems of economic development in *underdeveloped countries*. It has been generally assumed that this proportion tends to behave in a perverse way. This neutralises some of the favourable effects of increased productivity in agriculture and creates problems of financing the growth of non-agricultural activities. In this paper, an attempt is made to study the basis for this view. It must be emphasised that the argument of this paper is not that the problem of development in *underdeveloped areas* is capable of an easy solution because the marketed surplus doctrine is not correct. Rather, the object is to show that the problem of agriculture in these countries is one of the ways and means to increase productivity and not one of combating a peasant psychology which is no longer true.

The empirical results in Medani (1975) indicate that price is a significant determinant of marketing decisions of *subsistence crops* in traditional agriculture at all phases. Estimates of price coefficients range in magnitude from one phase to the other, but no specific pattern has emerged for the distribution of these coefficients. Marketable surplus is positively associated with market price at all phases.

An attempt is made by Hati (1976) to present certain non-linear mathematical relations between the marketable surplus of *paddy and farm-size*, as well as the marketable surplus of paddy and the net receipt of paddy. Attempt is also made to chart out a mathematical relation between the proportion of net receipt of marketable paddy and farm-size. Unlike in earlier work on this subject, what is taken note of is the marketable surplus and not the actually marketed surplus.

Narian's (1961) principal finding for the rural economy of India as a whole was that, "marketed surplus as a proportion of the value of produce declines up to 10-15 acres *size-group*, after which it records a steady 'increase'." Another significant result of his study was that farms below this level and those above it account for almost equal proportions of marketed surplus. This led him to conclude that, "Only half of the marketed surplus is what may be called a commercial surplus, while other half may be called a distress surplus".

Reddy (1987) carried out a study for marketable surplus of paddy by *size classes* in Andhra Pradesh whose results showed a larger proportion of marketable surplus for larger farmers. A similar study by Upender and Thirupathi (1998) in the same state had however a similar proportion of marketable surplus for all size classes. Ahmed and Arora (1999) differentiated between *fine and coarse winter paddy*, whereas Rangi (1993) and Parmod Kumar (1999) showed a very high proportion of marketed surplus of paddy for Punjab and Haryana respectively.

1.6 Modelling Marketed Surplus with Attributes[9]

Drawing from the Lancaster's theory of consumer choice (1966) the trait-based agricultural household model facilitates the formulation of the relationship between household production decisions and market participation choices.

The agricultural household maximises utility from the set of intrinsic quality attributes (z^C) of the crop it consumes (x), the consumption of an aggregate purchased good (g), and leisure (h), choosing the type and amount of crop it consumes and produces: $u[x(z^c), g, h|\Omega_{HH}, \Omega_M]$ where Ω_{HH} captures the heterogeneity in household characteristics. The household is constrained by its production and budget limitations (full income constraint), as well as by market imperfections. The production technology is defined by variable inputs, including the agronomic traits of crop planting material (z^P) and labour (l), used for the production of crop (q) from each variety i, on a pre-allocated, fixed amount of land: $q_i(z^P, l|\Omega_F, \Omega_M)$. The production technology is conditioned on the physical characteristics of the farm, denoted by Ω_F. The primary source of labour for crop production is typically the family (with total endowment of time for labour and leisure denoted by T). The number of distinct varieties existing in the village, denoted by V, represents the local stock (or endowment) of variety attributes. Although the bundles and levels of attributes provided by varieties are fixed from the perspective of an individual household, the household can vary the type and amount of

9. Edmeades *et al.*, 2004.

consumption and production attributes by changing the combination of varieties and quantities of planting material grown.

Household preferences and production choices are conditioned on market characteristics (Ω_M) as market imperfections can affect both consumer and producer behavior within the framework of non-separable decision-making Markets for crop may exist in domestic country. However, households are often located far from markets and the bulkiness of crop constraint market participation. Furthermore, premiums for quality differentials across varieties (concerning the taste rather than the size of the crop) are seldom observed, constraining the composition of participation. This is depicted by the tradability constraint for each variety i that the household grows, expressed as the difference between household output and consumption of bunches, or marketed surplus:

$$ms_i = q_i - x_i \qquad (1)$$

Although market failure is specific to households, it is binding for some varieties, with respect to which the household remains autarkic, i.e $ms_i = 0 \forall i \in not-traded$, while it is relaxed for other varieties, of which the household sells a proportion at the market, i.e. $ms_i \succ 0 \forall i \in traded$. Hence, while participation in markets is defined as a household-specific decision, composition of participation is expressed at the variety level.

Optimal levels of household consumption and output of i are defined, respectively, as $x_i = x_i(z^c, p_i, Y^*(z^p, p_i, \Omega_F, T, V, I) | \Omega_{HH}, \Omega_M)$ and household full income Y* is defined by production technology parameters (e.g. agronomic traits of planted varieties, banana bunch prices, farm characteristics), total endowments of time and stock of attributes, as well as exogenous sources of income, I. Aggregate goods are a numeraire commodity. Shadow values of family labour, planting material and non-traded varieties are functions of prices, household, farm and market characteristics, and total endowments of inputs (T and V). Crop prices are expressed as functions of attributes: $p_i(z^c, z^p)$ Combining the information, household output and consumption of i are given by:

$$q_i = q_i(z^p, p_i(z^c, z^p), V | \Omega_F, \Omega_M) \qquad (2)$$

$$x_i = x_i(z^c, z^p, p_i(z^c, z^p), T, V, I | \Omega_{HH}, \Omega_F, \Omega_M) \quad (3)$$

Recognising that agricultural households make consumption and production decisions simultaneously, and using the tradability constraint (1) and the expressions for crop produced (2) and consumed (3), the variety-specific marketed surplus is defined as a reduced-form function of attributes, other exogenous factors and a set of household, farm and market characteristics:

$$ms_i = ms_i(z^c, z^p, p_i, T, V, I | \Omega_{HH}, \Omega_F, \Omega_M) \quad (4)$$

This equation is the basis for the empirical analysis in the paper, and thus by us. Marketed surplus is measured as the number of measure of crop from variety i sold by households participating in crop markets.

1.6.1 Sluggish Marketed Surplus Combined with Positive Own Price Elasticity of Demand: A Paradoxical Result[10]

A key motivation for agricultural-household analysis which we discussed earlier is for policy analysis, based on comparative statics with theoretical or parameterised models. Analytically, agricultural household models resolve the apparent paradox of a positive own-price elasticity of demand for food in farm households, as well as the puzzle of sluggish marketed-surplus responses to food-price changes. Empirical models, using micro-survey data, have made it possible to estimate the magnitude of supply and marketed-surplus elasticity in a number of different country settings, while confirming quantitatively the importance of using household-farm, rather than simply "household" or "farm," models to analyse rural economies.

The fundamental difference between an agricultural household model and a pure consumer model is that, in the latter, the household budget is generally assumed to be fixed, whereas in household-farm models it is endogenous and depends on production decisions that contribute to income through farm profits. Thus, to the standard Slutsky effects of the consumer model, agricultural household models add an additional, "farm profit" effect, which may be positive (e.g., if the price of the home-produced staple increases) or negative (as

10. Taylor and Adelman, 2002

when the market wage increases, squeezing profits). In a consumer model, when the price of a normal good (say, food) increases, its demand unambiguously decreases: a negative "real income" effect reinforces a negative "substitution" effect, as illustrated in the most basic indifference-curve analysis. However, the household-farm is both a consumer and producer of food. As a consumer, it is adversely affected by a higher food price, but as producer, its profit from food production increases. This adds a positive "farm profit" effect to the negative Slutsky effects on food demand, pushing the budget constraint outward. If this profit effect outweighs the Slutsky effects, the household's demand for food increases with the food price. Indeed, out of seven empirical applications of the basic neoclassical household-farm model presented in Singh *et al.* (1986), four produced evidence of a positive own-price elasticity of food demand. This higher food demand dampens, and theoretically could reverse, a positive effect of food prices on the marketed surplus of food to urban households.

2

Gujarat Agriculture

A Macro Overview

2.1 Districts of Gujarat

The state was created in 1960 out of the 17 northern districts of the former Bombay State: Ahmedabad, Amreli, Banaskantha, Bharuch, Bhavnagar, Dang, Jamnagar, Junagadh, Kheda, Kachchh, Mehsana, Panchmahal, Rajkot, Sabarkantha, Surat, Surendranagar and Vadodara (Baroda).

In 1964, Gandhinagar district was formed from parts of Ahmedabad and Mehsana, and in 1966, Valsad district was split from Surat. On 2 October 1997, Anand district was split from Kheda, Dahod district was split from Panchmahal, Narmada district was split from Bharuch, Navsari district was split from Valsad and Porbandar district was split from Junagadh. In 2000 Patan district was formed from parts of Banaskantha and Mehsana. On 2 October 2007, Tapi is created as the state's 26 district. Gujarat now comprises 33 districts (Figure 2.1).

2.2 State Agricultural Profile

2.2.1 Climate

We use the Thornthwaite classification to classify climate in Gujarat. Devised by the American climatologist and geographer C. W. Thornthwaite, this climate classification method monitors the soil-water budget using evapotranspiration. It monitors the portion of total precipitation used to nourish vegetation over a certain area. It uses indices such as a humidity index and an aridity index to determine an area's moisture regime based upon its average temperature, average rainfall and average vegetation type. The moisture classification includes climatic classes with descriptors such as hyper-humid, humid,

Figure 2.1
Map of Districts of Gujarat

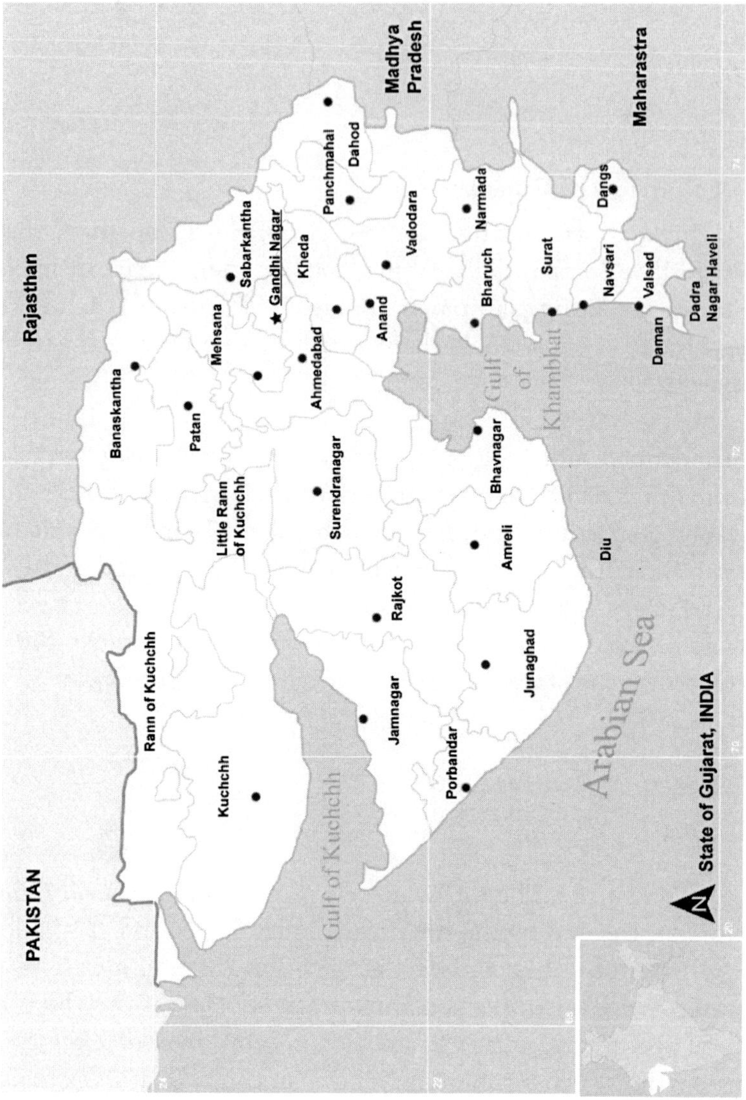

sub-humid, sub-arid, semi-arid and arid. Humid regions experience more precipitation than evaporation each year, while arid regions experience greater evaporation than precipitation on an annual basis. In terms of the standard climatic types, tropical climates *viz.*, sub-humid, arid and semi-arid are spread over different regions of the state. Out of total area of the state, 58.60 per cent fall under arid and semi-arid climatic zone. The arid zone contributes 24.94 per cent, while the semi-arid zone forms 33.66 per cent of the total area of the state. The regions in the extreme north comprising the district of Kachchh and the western parts of Banaskantha and Mehsana, the northern fringe of Saurashtra (Jamnagar) and its western part have arid climate; the rest of the state has semi-arid climate. The district of Valsad, Dangs, Surat, Vadodara and Kheda in the extreme south of the state have sub-humid climate.

2.2.2 Agro-Climatic Zones

South Gujarat (Heavy Rainfall Area): This region includes the whole of the Dangs, parts of Valsad district and parts of Surat district which have rainfall of 1,500 mm and more. The soil type is deep black with few patches of coastal alluvial, laterite and medium black soil. The crops grown are cotton, *jowar*, paddy, vegetables, horticultural crops and sugar cane.

South Gujarat (Moderate Rainfall Area): This region includes parts of Valsad, Surat and Bharuch districts; it has rainfall of 1,000-1,500 mm, the type of soil is deep black clayey soil. The crops grown are cotton, *jowar*, wheat, sugar cane and horticultural crops.

Middle Gujarat: This includes the areas between river Narmada and Vishwamitri including Panchmahal district, Vadodara district, part of Bharuch district and Borsad *taluka* of Kheda district. The rainfall level is of 800-1,000 mm. The soil is deep black, medium black to loamy sand. Crops grown include cotton, *bajra*, tobacco, pulses, wheat, paddy, maize, *jowar* and sugar cane.

North Gujarat: This is the area between rivers Vishwamitri and Sabarmati and part of Mehsana, Ahmedabad and Banaskantha districts including whole of Sabarkantha district, part of Ahmedabad district, whole of Kheda district, whole of Mehsana district and part of Banaskantha district. The rainfall level is between 625 and 875 mm. The soil type is sandy loamy to sandy soils. Crops grown are tobacco, wheat, *jowar*, minor millet, vegetables, oil seeds, spices and condiments.

Bhal and Coastal areas: This includes the area around the gulf of Khambhat and Bhal and coastal region in Bharuch and Surat districts, particularly,

1. Olpad *taluka* of Surat district.
2. Hansot and Wagra *talukas* of Bharuch district.
3. Dholka and Dhandhuka *talukas* of Ahmedabad district.
4. Vallabhipur and Bhavnagar *talukas* of Bhavnagar district.
5. Limbdi *taluka* of Suredranagar district.

The rainfall level is between 625 and 1,000 mm. Soil is medium black, poorly drained and saline. Crops are groundnut, cotton, *bajra*, dry wheat, pulses and *jowar*.

South Saurashtra: This region includes:

1. Whole of Junagadh district.
2. Part of Bhavnagar district (Sihor, Ghogha, Savarkundla, Gariadhar, Palitana, Talaja and Mahuva *talukas*).
3. Part of Amreli district (Dhari, Kodinar, Rajula, Jafrabad, Khambha, Amreli, Babra, Lilia, Lathi and Kunkavav *talukas*).
4. Part of Rajkot district (Jetpur, Dhoraji, Upleta and Gondal *talukas*).

The rainfall level is 625-750 mm. Soil is shallow medium black calcareous. Crops grown are groundnut, cotton, pulses, wheat, *bajra*, *jowar* and sugar cane.

North Saurashtra: This region includes:

1. Whole of Jamnagar district.
2. Part of Rajkot district (Padadhari, Lodhika, Jasdan, Rajkot, Wankaner, Morvi, Jamkandorna and Kotda Sangani *talukas*).
3. Part of Surendranagar district (Wadhvan, Muli, Chotila and Salya *talukas*).

4. Part of Bhavnagar district (Gadhada, Umrala and Botad *talukas*).

Rainfall is between 400-700 mm. The soil is shallow and medium black. The crops grown are groundnut, cotton, wheat, *bajra*, *jowar* and sugar cane.

North-West Zone: This region includes:

1. Whole of Kachchh district.
2. Malia *taluka* of Rajkot district.
3. Halvad, Dhrangadhra and Dasada *talukas* of Surendranagar district.
4. Sami, Harij and Chanasma *talukas* of Mehsana district.
5. Santalpur, Radhanpur, Kankrej, Diyodar Vav and Tharad *talukas* of Banaskantha district.
6. Viramgam and Daskroi city of Ahmedabad district.

The level of rainfall is 250-500 mm. With the type of soils being sandy and saline, the crops grown are cotton, *jowar*, groundnut, *bajra* and wheat.

Brief description of agro-climatic regions of Gujarat is presented in Table 2.1.

2.3 Structural Transformation of the State Agricultural Economy

The growth experience of Gujarat during the pre-reform period of 1980-1992 and the reform period of 1991-2004 is described below.

Identifying strengths and weaknesses, Gujarat was not a better performing state than the nation in terms of economic growth during the 1980s. It lagged behind the nation in almost all sectors. However, with increased speed of economic policy reforms in the post 1991-92 period, Gujarat improved in its growth performance remarkably. If growth acceleration in the post 1991-92 period is attributed to economic policy reforms at the national level, it is obvious that Gujarat has benefited from such reforms much more than other states. (Dholakia, 2007).

The share of agriculture in the state economy *vis-à-vis* other sectors in Gujarat has been low. It is not just recently that Gujarat has been considered a high growth state, its performance has always been better than the all-India in terms of economic growth.

Table 2.1

Agro-Climatic Regions of Gujarat

Region	*District*	*Rainfall (in mm)*	*Climate*	*Soils*
Southern Hills	Dangs, Valsad	1793	Semi-arid, dry sub-humid	Deep black coastal alluvium
Southern Gujarat	Surat, Bharuch	974	Semi-arid, dry sub-humid	Deep black coastal alluvium
Middle Gujarat	Baroda, Kheda, Panchmahal	904	Semi-arid	Medium black
North Gujarat	Ahmedabad, Gandhinagar, Mehsana, Sabarkantha, Banaskantha	735	Arid to semi-arid	Gray brown coastal alluvium
North West	Kachchh	340	Arid	Gray brown deltaic alluvium
North Saurashtra	Amreli, Bhavnagar, Jamnagar, Rajkot, Surendrangar	537	Semi-arid	Medium black calcareous
South Saurashtra	Junagadh	844	Dry sub-humid	Coastal alluvium, medium black

Source: Website of the Government of Gujarat, State Agricultural Profile. Department of Agriculture and Cooperation, Government of Gujarat.

Emphasis on development of commercial crops in the state has not resulted in higher incomes in the agricultural sector itself. There is therefore need for public investment in agriculture, in order to improve both productivity and incomes in the sector.

The share of the primary sector in state GDP had fallen to 19 per cent by 1999-2000, and this low proportion continued thereafter. This is a result of a decline in the absolute level of real agricultural output in the years following 1999-2000 and a simultaneous increase in output in the secondary and tertiary sectors.

While in India as a whole it is the services sector that has grown the fastest, the secondary sector has shown the most rapid growth in Gujarat.

On the other hand, the share of the tertiary sector in 2005-06 was 41.87 per cent, lower than the 50 per cent share of the sector at the all-India level.

The share of the primary as well as the secondary sectors is highly fluctuating in the state as compared to the all-India situation. The most obvious trend is the sharply declining one of the primary sector. The high fluctuations in the shares of the primary and secondary sectors are reflected in higher variance values in Gujarat than for the all-India data.

Prices have moved in favour of the agricultural sector. However, per capita income in the primary sector has always been the lowest of all three sectors. In the 1990s, the agricultural sector developed a closer relation with the secondary and tertiary sectors, from which it had been historically isolated in the state. The agricultural sector's role in an economy may be to provide agro-industrial inputs and/or wage goods (mainly food grains). Cotton, oil seeds and tobacco are especially important in the state. The share of high-value crops such as spices, fruit and vegetables in total output has increased after 1990-91. Agriculture's role, not as a wage good but as a provider of industrial inputs, becomes evident in the increased correlation between the agricultural and industrial sectors. This has however changed since 2002.

While demand from the secondary and tertiary sectors increased, demand from within the primary sector stagnated with declining incomes. The policy emphasis on agro-industry and commercial crops has not succeeded in increasing overall income of the primary sector. The agricultural sector has served to fuel economic growth in other sectors, but that economic growth has not fed into the sector itself.

After the 1980s, the Gujarat economy has progressed to the second stage of economic growth. However, the integral relationship between the agricultural and non-agricultural sectors still continues. The increased integration of the agricultural sector into the economy in the 1990s is likely to have been based on increased demand for agricultural inputs useful for agro-industry rather than on increased demand for wage goods. The years of the present decade are marked by an explosive growth in the agricultural sector. However, downturns in production still occur almost every alternate year.

In these circumstances, a vision of the agricultural sector as a dynamic sector and a sustained source of industrial growth, seems premature unless adequate steps are taken to weatherproof production. In light of the low relative incomes in the sector, there is a significant constraint on private investment in agriculture. This task will have to be undertaken through public investment.

A second and most important area of concern is that the agricultural sector, in spite of its relatively small contribution to state income, still continues to employ the largest proportion of workers. The sector is characterised by two trends: a rising agricultural price ratio and a declining per worker income level. These indicate that the higher relative agricultural prices have benefited a selective few farmers but not the majority in the agricultural sector. The orientation of the Agro Vision document is towards refocusing the agricultural sector as an industrial input provider, but this vision ignores the distributive aspect within the sector. Dynamic agricultural growth based on commercial crops—if stabilised and weatherproofed with the help of, irrigation—can be a source of increased incomes within the sector, but special efforts have to be made to see to it that the benefits of this growth are spread evenly within the sector (Dixit, 2009).

When we observe the Table 2.2, we realise that agriculture's share in national income has been falling in this decade in Gujarat.

Table 2.2

Sectoral Break-up of GSDP at Factor Cost at Constant (2004-05) Prices Percentage of GSDP: Gujarat: 2008 and 2011 and India 2008-2011

Sector	*3-year Average 2008-2011, (Gujarat)*	*3-year Average 2008-2011, (India)*
Gross State Domestic Product (GSDP)	100	100
Agriculture, forestry and fishing	12.8	14.4
Industry	41.1	28.3
Services	46.1	57.6

Source: Centre for Monitoring Indian Economy Pvt. Ltd.(CMIE) Database.

Clearly the share of services in Gujarat is lower than the rest of India and industry is dominant in Gujarat, comparatively.

2.4 Features of Growth of Crop Agriculture in Gujarat

Gujarat is significant in terms of area sown at the national level in *bajra*, maize, *tur*, onions, cabbages, brinjal and okra, bananas, papaya, chiku, groundnut, castor, *til*, cotton seed, fennel, cumin, fenugreek, *ajwain*, garlic, cotton and tobacco.

At the state level, the following crops are dominant in terms of area: rice, wheat, *bajra*, maize, potatoes, groundnut, cotton seed and cotton.

In terms of production at the national level, the production of the following crops in Gujarat is significant: *bajra*, *tur*, onions, brinjal, okra, bananas, papaya, chiku, groundnut, castor, til, cottonseed, fennel, cumin, fenugreek, ajwain, garlic, cotton and tobacco. Cropping pattern of Gujarat is shown in Table 2.3.

Up to early-1990s, *bajra* (pearl millet) and *jowar* (sorghum) were the main food grain crops, and cotton and groundnut were the main non-food crops. Area under cereals has declined from around 3,600 in 1990-91 to 3,400 hectare in the period 2006-2011. Area share of *bajra* that had remained constant at around 13 per cent till early-1990s has reduced to half in TE (triennium ending) 2009-10. Similarly, area under *jowar* declined from 6.2 per cent of GCA (gross cropped area) to only 1.3 per cent during this period. On the other hand, average area under wheat has more than doubled, from 5.7 lakh ha in TE 1992-93 to nearly 11 lakh ha in TE 2009-10 and now shares 34 per cent of the total cereal area. Area under rice has remained more or less stable at 5 to 6 per cent of the GCA. Acreage under groundnut that was 18 to 19 per cent of GCA throughout the 1980s, has declined to 15.8 per cent in the recent period. Substantial shifts in area under cotton have been witnessed during the post-reforms period, its share has improved considerably.

The share of cotton has reached 20.5 per cent by TE 2009-10. About 12.2 lakh ha of area has been diverted from other crops, mainly coarse cereals and pulses, towards cotton in the post-reform period.

Cropping pattern in the state has changed in favour of superior, more remunerative cereals like wheat and high-value crops such as oil seeds, cotton, spices, fruits and vegetables, floricultural and medicinal plants. Groundnut and cotton, being the main cash crops, have retained their dominant position in the cropping pattern. Area under coarse cereals has declined because of their lack of competitiveness over other crops. On the other hand, area under oil seeds such as castor, mustard and sesame has expanded significantly. In the recent period, cotton is rising fast.

Table 2.3

Cropping Pattern in Gujarat (Average Area and Production)

Crops	*Gross Area Sown of Particular Crop as % of All-India Gross Area Sown of this Crop (Average of 2001-02 to 2010-11)*	*Gross Area Sown Average of Particular Crop as % of State Gross Area Sown (Average 2001-02 to 2010-11)*	*Production of Particular Crop as % of All India Production of this Crop (Average 2001-02 to 2010-11)*
Food Grains	3.25	34.81	2.84
Cereals	3.19	27.77	2.77
Rice	1.59	6.05	1.36
Wheat	3.28	7.85	3.15
Coarse Cereals	5.51	13.88	5.59
Jowar	1.81	1.35	2.22
Bajra	9.58	7.85	13.46
Maize	6.29	4.21	4.23
Ragi	1.45		0.91
Small Millets	3.46		6.12
Pulses	3.5	7.04	3.86
Tur	7.92	2.48	9.84
Gram	2	1.27	2.15
Other Pulses	3.09	3.28	3.06
Vegetables, Roots and Tubers	5.27	0.91	5.61
Potatoes	2.96	3.56	4.03
Tomatoes	5.08		6.62
Onions and Other Vegetables	8.68		13.36
Onions	7.63		14.7
Edible Brassicas	6.67		5.79
Cabbages	7.83		6.36
Cauliflowers	5.53		5.27
Other Vegetables	5.56	1.41	4.99

contd...

...contd...

Brinjal	10.51		10.31
Okra	10.64		9.26
Bananas	8.38		13.68
Guavas	4.58		6.21
Mango	5.04		5.48
Citrus Fruits	4.13		4.71
Papaya	14.31		18.82
Other Fruits	5.64		7.52
Chiku	17.48		20.38
Pomegranates	4.07		5.94
Major Oil Seeds	11.37	25.52	14.89
Groundnut	31.32	16.75	36.52
Rapeseed and Mustard	4.49	2.35	5.77
Castor	46.24	3.09	70.88
Sesame (*Til*)	18.77	2.88	20.2
Cotton Seed	22.99	17.12	29.64
Spices and Condiments	13.47	3.42	11.38
Fennel Seed	81.29		89.04
Cumin Seed	51.45	1.69	55.14
Ginger	1.71		1.1
Fenugreek Seed	11.67		11.84
Chillies	1.16		
Ajwain	21.71		29.27
Garlic	16.1		22.63
Cotton	22.99	17.12	29.64
Sugar cane	4.39	1.7	4.83
Tobacco	19.2		21.66
All Crops	6.54	100	

Source: CMIE Database.

2.5 Recent Trends in Agricultural Production

Among the major food crops, the yield growth of *bajra* (at 2.3%) between 2001 and 2010 could not offset the declining acreage under it. The process of replacement of *bajra* by other crops gained momentum after 2000-01 (-4.53%) and is responsible for the entire fall in its output (at -2.3%). *Jowar* also recorded a decline in area growth (-0.53%). The production of *jowar* has also shown an upward trend despite productivity registering a slowdown after 2000.

Table 2.4 summarises the trends in area, production and yield for major crop cultivated in Gujarat.

Area under wheat has shown a statistically significant and phenomenal growth rate (10.7%) after 2000-01 and production has recorded an increase of 12.5 per cent per year. Yield levels have also improved significantly after 2000-01 (at 2.4% per annum) contributing to the unprecedented rise in its output.

Production of pulses during 2000-01 to 2010-11 has increased at the annual rate of 7.3 per cent (statistically significant). While the growth rate of area was modest at 1.6 per cent, its productivity showed a considerable breakthrough rising at 6 per cent. Among other food crops, potato, fruits & vegetables and spices (mainly chilly) have registered fairly high growth rates.

The annual growth rates for spices from 1990-91 onwards were modest. After 2000-01, the growth rate for spices was as high as 19.3 per cent. Output of potato has nearly doubled in the post-liberalisation phase. Gujarat is a major groundnut-producing state; its average contribution to the total production in the country is 37 per cent. In the post-liberalisation phase, even though groundnut acreage is facing stagnation or replacement by other crops, its yield performance is better owing to several years of good rainfall that facilitates early sowing. Overall, the output of oil seeds in Gujarat is growing at a high rate of 4.1 per cent almost entirely driven by the productivity growth (4.8%).

Cotton is currently the single most important non-food crop of Gujarat. There has been a marked improvement in cotton production in post-liberalisation phase. After 2000-01, area under cotton increased at the rate of 5.3 per cent and its productivity grew at 11.4 per cent. During the period 2000-01 to 2010-11, growths in area and productivity have combined to cause production growth rate of 15.4 per cent. The single most important factor driving this growth is the widespread adoption of Bt cotton.

Tobacco is a minor crop in the Gujarat economy (claiming less than 1% of GCA), but is an important crop for the districts of Central Gujarat. The average productivity of tobacco is decreasing steadily.

The growth performance for major crops reveals that the post-liberalisation phase was marked by improvements in yield levels for all the major food crops, groundnut and cotton. Food grains as a category recorded a decline in acreage up to 2000-01. Between 2001 and 2010, the share of food grain area in GCA stabilised at around 34 per cent. While *bajra*, *jowar* and maize recorded a decline in acreage growth, wheat area expanded very rapidly (estimated to be 10.7% annually) that arrested the falling importance of food grains in the agricultural economy of the state. Commercialisation process and crop diversification towards non-food crops (cotton, spices, horticulture) are positive developments. Castor and sesame besides groundnut are the other commercial crops that are amenable to processing and have expanding domestic and global demand (Mehta, 2012a).

Table 2.4

Trend of Shift in Area, Production and Productivity in Gujart

Crop		*1961-1970 (Av.)*	*1971-1980 (Av.)*	*1981-1990 (Av.)*	*1991-2000 (Av.)*	*2000-01*	*2001- 02*	*2002-03*	*2003-04*	*2004-05*	*2005-06*	*2006-07*
Cereals	A	44.62	44	41.56	36.54	29.75	30.8	30.2	32	29.5	31.9	34.2
	P	24.88	36.07	42.05	46.48	29.36	48.3	40.3	59.5	46.7	57.2	71.3
	Y	558	820	1011	1272	986	1567	1335	1496	1583	1795	2085
Pulses	A	4.79	5.44	8.76	8.98	7.42	7.79	7.49	8.33	7.1	8.06	9.42
	P	1.68	2.35	5.18	5.65	2.49	4.22	3.66	6.22	4.81	5.87	7.58
	Y	350	432	591	629	336	542	489	747	678	728	804
Oil seeds	A	22.24	22.24	25.8	29.05	28.6	28.6	29	29.7	29.8	30	33.7
	P	12.54	17.5	21.33	27.85	17.38	37.5	18.8	56.6	29	44.9	49.9
	Y	563	787	827	959	608	1309	648	1907	973	1496	1484
Cotton	A	17.39	19.05	13.1	13.86	16.75	17.4	16.7	16.4	29.8	20.8	20.3
	P	15.48	19.46	16.18	23.86	12.83	16.8	18.8	40.3	29	73.8	75
	Y	151	174	210	293	130	165	191	417	165	604	627
Tobacco	A	0.89	0.99	1.25	1.39	1.13	1.1	1.28	0.68	0.71	1.14	1.03
	P	0.82	1.51	2.08	2.42	1.86	1.79	2.27	1.25	1.14	2.09	1.98
	Y	921	1525	1664	1741	1653	1621	1767	1831	1597	1833	1922
Sugar cane (Jaggery)	A	0.31	0.6	1.2	2.05	2.57	2.66	2.52	1.76	1.97	1.97	1.89
	P	1.78	4.05	8.59	15.75	18.18	17.1	17.6	12.7	14.6	14.6	14.6
	Y	5741	6750	7158	7682	7073	6407	6966	7182	7407	7407	7740

Note: A= area in lakh ha, P= production in lakh MT, Y= yield Kg/ha.

Source: Website of the Agriculture and Cooperation Department, Government of Gujarat.

3

Empirical Analysis

3.1 Sample Farmer Profile

As a prerequisite to our main analysis, it remains customary to bricfly describe some characteristic features of the sample households we deal with in this study, which in turn facilitates greater understanding of the socio economic backdrop of the population. Table 3.1 describes general characteristics of the sample households. An interesting characteristic we observe is that the average age of the decision-maker is close to 50, this clearly shows that as with general census households, farming families are headed in this area by middle-aged males. Marginal farmers head of the household is even older at 62 years. The fact that farm household size is more than 4-5 persons as in the census implies that family is not nuclear but is larger. The average size is 6.7. The size of households of marginal and large farms is above 7. Large farmers can support a large family size. Marginal farmers have a low land base but the family members depend on agriculture. The main occupation is crop farming throughout and dairying dominates as a subsidiary occupation (86%) with service (4.6%), farm labour (1.85%) and others (7.4%) also being subsidiary occupations. Dairying is a subsidiary and important occupation in rural India now and this is particularly true for Gujarat. This is more so for Central Gujarat and districts like Kheda and Vadodara as compared to districts in Saurashtra. There are also areas where, in migration of farm labour from the tribal districts of Eastern and Southern Gujarat and Maharashtra is common, hence smaller farm labour enumeration at household level.

As would be expected, years of schooling increase with family size. There are more males than females in the families. In terms of caste composition, general category predominates, followed by OBC (other backward class) and then SC (scheduled caste); in fact, the general category proportion is much higher in large farms which would imply operational ownership of landed property by the upper castes in most prosperous tracts in Gujarat, though this requires further detailed study to confirm the phenomena.

Table 3.1

Characteristics of Sampled Farmers

Characteristics Categories	*Marginal*	*Small*	*Medium*	*Large*	*All Farms*
Average Age of decision maker (yrs)	62	49.92	48.79	47.58	48.9
Subsidiary Occupation					
Dairy (%)					86.11
Service (%)					4.629
Farm labour (%)					1.85
Others (%)					7.41
Education (years of schooling)	6.35	7.8	8.15	9.53	8.61
Family Size (no.)	7.14	5.88	6.53	7.01	6.70
Males	3.92	3.11	3.52	3.63	3.55
Females	3.21	2.77	2.91	3	2.95
Social Grouping					
SC (%)					9.74
ST (%)					1.11
OBC (%)					33.14
General (%)					55.15
Others (%)					.8
All (%)	1.39	7.52	50.97	40.11	100

3.1.1 Operational Holding Characteristics

Our study shows that irrigation provision by Sardar Sarovar Project (SSP) has led to a major trend of what is called reverse tenancy. Smaller farmers have leased out land to larger farmers. Because a major part of the area covered in this study falls in the Command Area of the Sardar Sarovar Project, more than 90 per cent of the operational holdings are irrigated. This area has moderate rainfall and has alternate sources for irrigation, also investment has been made for irrigation sources. Since the districts chosen are in those areas of Gujarat like Vadodara and Kheda which fall under the Narmada command or are otherwise having access to some irrigation sources a very large proportion of the land is irrigated. Broadly only leasing in is seen (very little leasing out) and all this leased-in land is irrigated, this seems obvious because only irrigated land would be leased in. Clearly the land that entered into the lease market (leased-in land) has come out from small farmers in irrigated tracts. Table 3.2 is a descriptive statistics of operational land holding pattern for the sample. Large farm households lease in 2.59 ha of irrigated land per household, as compared to 1.23 ha per household for all households. This is also understandable considering the fact that the irrigated tracts will have a greater demand in the lease market as compared to un-irrigated tracts. This is an area of what is called 'reverse tenancy.' In other words, smaller farmers lease out land to middle and large farms and join the landless labour force. It is to be noted in this context that against popular belief, the larger farms in these highly productive land stretches are observed to lease-in land instead of leasing-out, which in turn indicates towards development of capitalist type of farming on large plots of land. Ever since B.B. Patel's well-known study in the 1970s, it is well known that leasing in is a major characteristic of the reorganisation of land in Gujarat. This has been accentuated by SSP. This requires further study. The study also shows that medium and large farms which dominate this study also cultivate the largest proportion of operational holding. The study has 5 marginal farmers, 27 small farmers, 183 medium farmers and 144 large farmers. (Note here that some of the *bajra* and wheat households are common thus explaining the distribution across sample sizes in Table 3.2 aggregating to greater than total sample size.) We also observe that the distribution of farmers by size class across crops reflects this larger farmer bias in our sample.

Medium and large farmers have leased in more irrigated land, what we described as reverse tenancy.

3.1.2 Area

In terms of percentage of gross cropped area (GCA), cotton (12.63%) is a major crop during *kharif* and wheat (21.84%) in *rabi* season. Paddy and vegetables are other important crops grown in *kharif* season. Area is also being allocated to other crops like tobacco and potato. As far as *rabi* season is concerned, wheat is grown on 21.84

Table 3.2

Average Operational Holding Characteristics (Average per Household in Hectare)

Categories	*No. of Farmers*	*Owned Land*		*Leased in*		*Leased out*		*Operational Holding*	
		Irrigated	*Un-irrigated*	*Irrigated*	*Un-irrigated*	*Irrigated*	*Un-irrigated*	*Irrigated*	*Un-irrigated*
					Overall				
Marginal	5	0.43	0.27	0	0	0	0	0.43	0.27
Small	27	1.3	0.14	0	0	0	0	1.21	0.09
Medium	183	4.5	0.64	0.38	0.03	0.01	0.08	4.73	0.45
Large	144	15.28	2.2	2.59	0	0.14	0	17.61	2.11
All Farms	359	8.53	1.22	1.23	0.02	0.06	0.04	9.57	1.09
					Tur				
Marginal	3	0.27	0.44	0	0	0	0	0.27	0.44
Small	10	1.07	0.37	0	0	0	0	1.07	0.24
Medium	43	3.24	1.79	0.83	0.13	0	0.33	3.87	1.19
Large	44	14.5	2.52	4.06	0	0.23	0	17.95	2.35
All Farms	100	7.89	1.93	2.14	0.05	0.1	0.14	9.68	1.58
					Wheat				
Marginal	2	0.66	0	0	0	0	0	0.66	0
Small	14	1.44	0	0	0	0	0	1.3	0
Medium	95	4.89	0.28	0.24	0	0.02	0	4.99	0.22
Large	69	15.62	2.06	1.94	0	0.1	0	17.46	2
All farms	259	8.77	0.95	0.88	0	0.05	0	9.53	0.89
					Bajra				
Marginal	2	0.66	0	0	0	0	0	0.66	0
Small	17	1.44	0	0	0	0	0	1.3	0
Medium	107	4.48	0.36	0.31	0	0.03	0	4.62	0.29
Large	53	14.23	1.76	1.51	0	0.19	0	15.55	1.7
All farms	179	7.04	0.74	0.63	0	0.07	0	7.5	0.68

per cent of the land. This is traditionally an area where paddy and wheat farming was giving way to oil seeds and commercial crops. SSP seems to have made the return to paddy and wheat. SSP water is at the present stage uncontrolled at the delivery level and flood irrigation leads to paddy and wheat farming dominating. Cotton farming as we saw in the earlier sections on Gujarat agriculture has been very successful on account of the new Bt technology and it has spearheaded Gujarat's agricultural growth in the last decade and a half. Marginal farmers only grow paddy, other cereals and pulses, which is expected from the subsistence nature of activity in very small holdings.

Table 3.3

Cropping Pattern

(Area in ha)

Crops Categories	*Marginal*	*Small*	*Medium*	*Large*	*All Farms*
Kharif					
Paddy	0.12	1.64	46.73	43.46	91.95
% to GCA	2.83	7.99	8.47	3.59	5.15
Other Cereals	1.38	4.93	105.98	95.53	207.83
% to GCA	33.37	24.06	19.21	7.89	11.63
Pulses	0.52	3.03	28.39	76.35	108.30
% to GCA	12.59	14.76	5.15	6.31	6.06
Oilseeds		0.58	32.06	83.85	116.49
% to GCA		2.82	5.81	6.93	6.52
Cotton		0.81	39.04	185.85	225.69
% to GCA		3.95	7.08	15.35	12.63
Vegetables		0.00	5.50	14.10	19.61
% to GCA		0.00	1.00	1.16	1.10
Other crops		0.46	80.19	255.65	336.31
% to GCA		2.25	14.54	21.12	18.82
Rabi					
Wheat		1.74	88.24	300.26	390.23
% to GCA		8.47	15.99	24.80	21.84

Oilseeds, cotton, vegetables and fruits are all grown largely on medium and large farms. Commercialisation is therefore more in such farms.

3.1.3 Production

Output outcomes follow from area allocations, particularly of irrigated area. Sardar Sarovar canal irrigation has also led to a resurgence of *kharif* paddy.

Table 3.4

Cropping Pattern: Total Production in Each Size Category (qtl)

Crops	*Marginal*	*Small*	*Medium*	*Large*	*All Farms*
Kharif					
Paddy	1.0	56.0	1884.2	1321.0	3262.2
Other Cereals	18.0	13.6	483.0	396.0	910.6
Pulses	9.2	15.3	215.1	756.6	996.1
Oilseeds		10.4	483.8	1266.2	1760.4
Cotton		7.6	659.0	3165.9	3832.5
Other crops		5.0	866.8	5836.4	6708.2
Rabi – Wheat		53.6	2590.6	6070.0	8714.2
Summer – *Bajra*	10.4	110.4	2039	3133	5292.8

Major output consequences are in medium and large farms, taking the agricultural year as a whole, wheat emerges in quantity terms as the largest crop. Marginal farms in our sample don't grow wheat. Small farms grow 53.6 qtl, but large farms grow 6,070 qtl and medium farms 2,590.6 qtl. This is noteworthy, because cereals were falling as a proportion of Gujarat agriculture in earlier decades. SSP has as we have shown led to this reversal. Small farms grow only 7.6 qtl of cotton as compared to 659 qtl by medium farms and 3,165.9 qtl from large farms. SSP has as we have shown led to this reversal (Table 3.4). Another noteworthy crop is cotton, in which the performance is driven by technology. Groundnut was an important crop in Gujarat and castor too in the 1990s.

Generally across farm size categories, yield tends to not fluctuate too much. It is interesting that the relation between farm size and productivity still shows that in some crops, small farms hold out in their performance. This aspect will be studied more in the econometric analysis of this study.

Table 3.5

Production (Values in Quintal per Hectare)

Crops	*Marginal*	*Small*	*Medium*	*Large*	*All Farms*
Kharif					
Paddy		34.175	40.320	30.394	35.478
Other Cereals		2.757	4.557	4.145	4.382
Pulses		5.039	7.574	9.909	9.198
Oilseeds		17.975	15.090	15.101	15.112
Cotton		9.392	16.882	17.035	16.981
Other crops		10.840	10.809	22.829	19.947
Rabi - Wheat		30.880	29.359	20.216	22.331
Summer - *Bajra*		28.936	28.118	33.794	31.108

3.1.4 Source of Irrigation

Electric tube wells are the major source of irrigation; in some areas, diesel tube wells and bore wells are also used for irrigation. This shows that there is sufficient supply of electricity for irrigation. Our sample shows that investment in tube wells is high. There is a great thrust for water in Gujarat agriculture and this continues with SSP water. There are many areas of over-exploitation and these are called 'grey areas' in our sample areas. Since SSP water supply is not controlled, paddy cultivation is done with canal water. If the farmer is a tail ender in the canal and gets little water, *tur* is cultivated instead of paddy. In Table 3.6, sources of irrigation are shown.

3.1.5 Farm Machinery

Use of farm machines is constrained by considerations of profitability; a large amount of expenditure on tractors, tube wells and threshing machines was seen by farmers in these areas, indicating prosperity. High expense on an average on tractors and tube wells is seen, indicating sufficient purchase and use by medium and large farmers. Table 3.7 shows use of machinery for the sample households.

Table 3.6

Source of Irrigation (Crop-wise and Source-wise Distribution of Irrigated Area in Different Size Classes)

(% Area under Irrigation)

Crops	*Marginal*	*Small*	*Medium*	*Large*	*All Farms*
Kharif - Paddy					
Canal	0.00	0.00	11.44	2.64	7.40
Electric tube well	0.00	71.60	88.04	94.07	90.32
Bore well	0.00	0.00	1.56	3.29	2.28
Others	0.00	28.40	4.42	0.00	2.99
Kharif - Other Cereals					
Canal	0.00	2.57	4.59	1.60	3.16
Electric tube well	15.81	44.24	85.01	95.48	89.13
Bore well	84.19	36.70	5.95	2.65	5.05
Kharif - Pulses					
Canal	0.00	7.93	40.58	17.23	22.64
Electric tube well	100.00	29.90	40.85	28.99	31.96
Bore well	0.00	50.21	22.53	36.39	33.41
Others	0.00	11.96	10.95	4.87	6.58

Table 3.7

Farm Machinery (Average Investment of Different Machinery per Household and Hectare)

Crops	*Average Investment per Farm (₹)*			*Average Investment per Hectare (₹)*		
Farm Class	*Tractors*	*Threshing Machine*	*Tube Well*	*Tractors*	*Threshing Machine*	*Tube Well*
Marginal	0	0	20000	0	0	28818
Small	0	0	24074	0	0	18487
Medium	62502	7180	81530	12069	1386	15743
Large	183006	10444	160416	9281	529	8135
All Farms	105267	7849	107994	9878	736	10134

3.1.6 Livestock

Maintaining cattle/buffalo is not a viable proposition for the smaller farms, as their use has become extremely confined in the face of competition from tractors under modern cultivation practices. Livestock and fodder costs have also become high.

Across all size classes, livestock other than cattle/buffalo is not kept, as the average number of ruminants is quite low which confirms their prohibitive costs.

Across all sizes, farmer households have large per hectare cattle holding since dairying is a major source of livelihood. Of course, medium and large farms have larger herd size. Small farms maintain much larger herd size in relation to their land holding. Livestock per household in large farms is high; this is a feature which results naturally in societies where number of cattle owned is seen as a sign of wealth. Table 3.8 shows livestock per household and per hectare among different categories of farmers.

Table 3.8

Farm Size and Livestock

Farm Class	*Cattle (per hh)*	*Cattle (per ha)*	*Buffalo (per hh)*	*Buffalo (per ha)*	*Others (per hh)*	*Others (per ha)*
Marginal	0.20	0.29	1.40	2.02	0.00	0.00
Small	0.89	0.68	0.89	0.68	0.33	0.26
Medium	1.43	0.28	1.50	0.29	0.16	0.03
Large	2.09	0.11	2.97	0.15	0.37	0.02
All Farms	1.64	0.15	2.04	0.19	0.25	0.02

3.1.7 Sale Price

Pulses have a sale price of above 3200/qtl except in small farms where it is lower than 3000/qtl. Oilseeds also have the same range of sale price/qtl, with small farmers selling at 3000/qtl. Cotton across farm size sells at above 3700/qtl. Vegetables sell for about 10 times as much though there is variation in the price across and within size classes. *Kharif* paddy sells for around ₹ 1000/qtl. *Rabi* wheat sells for more than ₹ 1000/qtl. Small farmers get lower prices around 10-25 per cent lower than large farmers. There are exceptions in data like in vegetables where medium farmers seem to be growing higher value added vegetables and large farmers, low value added. The major feature which emerges is the better terms received in the market by medium and large farmers. The impression that in Gujarat cooperative institutions lead to improved terms for small and marginal farms is not borne out by this study. Table 3.9 briefly explains average sale price for different produces among the sample.

Table 3.9

Average Sale Price (₹/qtl) Received for Different Crops

Crops	*Marginal*	*Small*	*Medium*	*Large*	*All Farms*
Kharif					
Paddy		938	998	1212	1051
Pulses*	3000	2783	3379	3226	3262
Oilseeds		3000	3207	3275	3233
Cotton		3863	3743	4002	3899
Vegetables			47156	5818	24420
Other crops		5500	3163	3025	3110
Rabi - Wheat		1019	1099	1167	1124

Note: *For marginal category ₹3000/qtl.

3.1.8 Production and Availability of Crop by Farm Size

For all crops, there is hardly any beginning stock per household at an average, the larger two farm sizes have higher average production in the season, i.e., large farmers produce more. Production clearly rises with farm size. In *tur* medium farmer households grow 9.41 qtl per households and large farmer household grow 16.73 qtl. In wheat, these figures are 24.04 qtl and 76.12 qtl respectively. *Bajra* is grown by marginal farms but only 9.46 qtl per household. The numbers for small farm households are slightly higher at 11.76 qtl but those of medium farm are 27.78 qtl and of large farm households are 81.41 qtl (Table 3.10).

3.1.9 Sale Pattern and Realised Price of Selected Crops

Purchase Agencies and the Share They Buy from Size Class of Farms

Average sale is approximately 7 qtl for *tur*, 46 qtl for wheat and 40 qtl for *bajra*. *Tur* sales are 1 to approximately 2 qtl per farm for marginal and small farms. These are 4.09 and 10.85 for medium and large farm households respectively. In wheat the differences are more. Small farms sell 3.6 qtl per household, but medium farms sell 22.85 qtl and large farms 73.47 qtl.

Table 3.10

Availability of Crop by Farm Size

(in qtl/hh)

Crop	*Farm Size*	*Average Beginning Stock*	*Average Production*	*Net Average Availability*
Tur	Marginal	0.00	3.16	3.16
	Small	0.00	2.07	2.07
	Medium	0.03	9.41	9.44
	Large	0.48	16.73	17.21
	All farms	0.23	11.66	11.88
Wheat	Marginal	0.00	0.00	0.00
	Small	0.00	6.91	6.91
	Medium	0.06	24.04	24.1
	Large	0.40	76.12	76.52
	All farms	0.20	45.03	45.22
Bajra	Marginal	0.00	9.46	9.46
	Small	0.00	11.78	11.78
	Medium	0.10	27.78	27.88
	Large	0.01	81.41	80.56
	All farms	0.06	42.10	41.90

Sales are generally to private trader/money lender and increase monotonically by size. Average price received per quintal by private trader is ₹ 2,500-3,500 in *tur*, ₹ 880-1,100 in wheat and ₹ 500-800 in *bajra*. The processor or millers and private companies work on a commission basis in processing *dals* (Table 3.11).

Table 3.11

Sale Pattern and Realised Price of Selected Crops

Farm Class	*Average Sale in qtl. per farm*	*Percentage of Sales*			*Avg. Price Received by Farmer*		
		Pvt. Trader / Money lender	*Processor/ Miller*	*Pvt. Company*	*Pvt. Trader / Money lender*	*Processor/ Miller*	*Pvt. Company*
			Tur				
Marginal	2.4	100.00	0.00	0.00	2750.00		
Small	1.02	100.00	0.00	0.00	3550.00		
Medium	4.09	85.67	0.46	13.87	3165.63	2800.00	3450.00
Large	10.85	82.16	2.05	15.79	3140.00	3800.00	2866.67
All farms	6.71	83.54	1.59	14.88	3150.00	3300.00	3012.50

Farm Class	*Average Sale in qtl per farm*	*Percentage of Sales*			*Avg. Price Received by Farmer*		
		Pvt. Trader / Money lender	*Processor/ Miller*	*Pvt. Company*	*Pvt. Trader / Money lender*	*Processor/ Miller*	*Pvt. Company*
			Wheat				
Marginal	0.00	0.00	0.00	0.00			
Small	3.60	100.00	0.00	0.00	1100.00		
Medium	22.85	85.60	2.40	0.12	1098.33	1000	1000
Large	73.47	69.88	23.82	0.72	1153.24	1275	1000
All farms	45.40	73.94	18.32	0.56	1124.17	1137.5	1000

Farm Class	*Average Sale in qtl per farm*	*Percentage of Sales*			*Avg. Price Received by Farmer*		
		Govt Agent	*Processor/ Miller*	*Pvt. Company*	*Govt Agents*	*Processor/ Miller*	*Pvt. Company*
			Bajra				
Marginal	6.00	0.00	0.00	100.00	-	-	1100
Small	8.98	3.34	96.66	0.00	1200.00	850.00	-
Medium	24.43	22.22	69.85	7.94	950.00	917.35	912.5
Large	72.60	52.64	47.36	0.00	934.29	978.57	-
All farms	39.47	41.54	55.70	2.76	947.89	925.95	950

3.1.10 Crop Retention Pattern

Generally retention rises with farm size. In the case of *tur*, retention of marginal and small farmers is around a third of large farmer households. Medium farmers also have a slightly higher retention than marginal and small farms. *Tur dal* is an item of self-consumption and probably has a high income elasticity of demand. Large farm households also purchase *oil seeds dal* to a much larger extent. In Table 3.12, we show crop retention pattern.

Table 3.12

Crop Retention Pattern

Farm Size	*Self-Consumption*			*Seeds in qtls/Hh*	*Total Retention qtls/Hh*
	Retention qtls/Hh	*Purchased*			
		qtls/Hh	*Price*		
		Tur			
Marginal	0.43	0.00	0.00	0.21	0.64
Small	0.49	0.06	1700.00	0.03	0.52
Medium	0.74	0.14	1104.65	0.06	0.80
Large	1.86	0.51	534.09	0.29	2.17
All farms	1.20	0.29	848.48	0.17	1.37

Farm Size	Self-Consumption			Seeds in	Total Retention
	Retention qtls/Hh	Purchased		qtls/Hh	qtls/Hh
		qtls/Hh	Price		
		Wheat			
Marginal	0.00	0.00	0.00	0.00	0.00
Small	2.22	0.43	264.70	0.11	2.33
Medium	4.23	0.36	146.42	0.32	4.84
Large	9.20	0.31	99.00	1.85	11.53
All farms	5.98	0.34	134.74	0.89	7.22
		Bajra			
Marginal	5.20	3.00	425.00	0.00	5.20
Small	5.23	0.47	108.82	0.06	5.59
Medium	7.51	0.29	100.46	0.09	8.77
Large	14.02	0.36	73.58	0.08	18.89
All farms	9.20	0.36	96.90	0.08	11.42

3.1.11 Crop Losses

Interestingly, small farmers have a significant proportion of losses. It should also be mentioned here that crop loss in harvesting depends much upon factors like the state of maturity of crops, timing of harvesting, unwanted rainfall in the maturity period, distance of plot from farmhouse, etc. This study does not take into account such factors separately and provides the overall estimate of crop loss during harvesting. Table 3.13 summarises crop loss during production/ processing of crop.

Table 3.13

Crop Losses (in kg) in Percentage of Total Physical Losses and as % of Total Production by Mode

Farm Class	Harvesting		Threshing		Winnowing		Loss due to Animals		Overall Loss	
	% Loss in Produ ction	% in Total Loss	% Loss in Produ ction	% in Total Loss	% Loss in Produ ction	% in Total Loss	% Loss in Produ ction	% in Total Loss	% Loss in Produ ction	% in Total Loss
					Tur					
Marginal	2.11	74	0	0	0.74	25.9	0	0	2.85	100
Small	7.73	33.4	0.58	2.51	1.88	8.14	12.94	55.95	23.13	100
Medium	4.33	29.02	1.18	9.1	0.52	4.02	7.53	57.87	13.56	100
Large	5.33	30.54	1.08	6.18	0.64	3.67	10.38	59.61	17.44	100
All Farms	5	30.24	1.1	6.91	0.62	3.92	9.34	58.93	16.06	100
					Wheat					
Marginal	0	0	0	0					0	100
Small	1.41	60.47	0.92	39.53					2.33	100
Medium	2.64	84.49	0.49	15.51					3.14	100
Large	2.86	85.4	0.5	14.6					3.36	100
All Farms	2.79	85.03	0.5	14.97					3.29	100

			Bajra			
Marginal	3.96	49.34	4.07	50.66	8.03	100
Small	1.69	48.64	1.79	51.36	3.48	100
Medium	2.31	65.89	1.2	34.11	3.51	100
Large	1.72	65.5	0.9	34.5	2.62	100
All Farms	1.96	65.05	1.05	34.95	3.01	100

Note: In *Tur*, apart from marginal farmers, there is greater than 15 per cent loss in production overall, in *bajra* and wheat it is much less.

3.1.12 Crop Losses during Transport

Transport losses from field to floor and floor to market are basically while transporting through tractor. Crop losses occur during transport of crop output. This happens mainly during transporting harvested crop from field to threshing floor and transporting stored crop from farm to market.

Losses are generally attained while transporting through tractor that being the dominant mode of transportation; some losses are also attained while transporting by person on head, as well as by animal. Losses in packing are during packing in bags. Table 3.14 shows crop loss during transportation.

Table 3.14

Crop Losses during Transport of All Farm Total Losses in Each Mode as % of Total Losses and % of Production

			Loss by Mode of Transport from Field to Floor			
Mode	*Head*		*Tractor*		*Overall*	
	Loss % out of overall total Prodn.	*% in Total Loss*	*Loss % out of overall total Prodn.*	*% in Total Loss*	*Loss % out of overall total Prodn.*	*% in Total Loss*
Tur						
Overall	0.03	23.12	0.11	48.19	0.5	100
			Loss by Mode of Packing from Field to Floor			
Mode	*Bags*		*Overall*			
	Loss % out of overall total Prodn.	*% in Total Loss*	*Loss % out of overall total Prodn.*	*%in Total Loss*		
Tur						
Overall	0.15	100	0.5	100		
			Loss by Mode of Transport from Floor to Market			
Mode	*Head*	*Tractor*	*Overall*			
	Loss % out of overall total Prodn.	*% in Total Loss*	*Loss % out of overall total Prodn.*	*% in Total Loss*	*Loss % out of overall total Prodn.*	*% in Total Loss*
Tur						
Overall	0.03	23.12	0.11	48.19	0.5	100

contd...

		Loss by Mode of Packing from Floor to Market				
Mode	*Bags*	*Overall*				
	Loss % out of overall total Prodn.	*% in Total Loss*	*Loss % out of overall total Prodn.*	*%in Total Loss*		
Tur						
Overall	0.15	100	0.5	100		
		Loss by Mode of Transport from Field to Floor				
Mode	*Tractor*	*Overall*				
	Loss % out of overall total Prodn.	*% in Total Loss*	*Loss % out of overall total Prodn.*	*% in Total Loss*		
Wheat						
Overall	0.01	100	0.01	100		
		Loss by Mode of Packing from Field to Floor				
Mode	*Bags*	*Overall*				
	Loss % out of overall total Prodn.	*%in Total Loss*	*Loss % out of overall total Prodn.*	*% in Total Loss*		
Wheat						
Overall	0.01	100	0.01	100		
		Loss by Mode of Transport from Floor to Market				
Mode	*Tractor*	*Overall*				
	Loss % out of overall total Prodn.	*% in Total Loss*	*Loss % out of overall total Prodn.*	*% in Total Loss*		
Wheat						
Overall	0.01	100	0.01	100		
		Loss by Mode of Packing from Floor to Market				
Mode	*Bags*	*Overall*				
	Loss % out of overall total Prodn.	*% in Total Loss*	*Loss % out of overall total Prodn.*	*% in Total Loss*		
Wheat						
Overall	0.01	100	0.01	100		
		Loss by Mode of Transport from Field to Floor				
Mode						
	Animal	*Tractor*	*Overall*			
	Loss % out of overall total Prodn.	*% in Total Loss*	*Loss % out of overall total Prodn.*	*% in Total Loss*	*Loss % out of overall total Prodn.*	*% in Total Loss*
Bajra						
Overall	0.01	36.14	0.01	63.86	0.02	100
		Loss by Mode of Packing from Field to Floor				
Mode	*Bags*	*Overall*				
	Loss % out of overall total Prodn.	*% in Total Loss*	*Loss % out of overall total Prodn.*	*% in Total Loss*		
Bajra						
Overall	0.02	100	0.02	100		
		Loss by Mode of Transport from Floor to Market				
Mode	*Animal*	*Tractor*	*Overall*			
	Loss % out of overall total Prodn.	*% in Total Loss*	*Loss % out of overall total Prodn.*	*% in Total Loss*	*Loss % out of overall total Prodn..*	*% in Total Loss*
Bajra						
Overall	0	5.35	0.02	94.65	0.03	100

contd...

...contd...

Loss by Mode of Packing from Floor to Market						
Mode						
	Bags	*Overall*				
	Loss % out of overall total Prodn.	*% in Total Loss*	*Loss % out of overall total Prodn.*	*% in Total Loss*		
Bajra						
Overall	0.03	100	0.03	100		

3.2 Factors Influencing Marketed Surplus

3.2.1 Distance and Type of Market

A greater proportion (60%) of household sell in local market across farm sizes. However, around 40 per cent of households sell in distant markets. The farmers generally prefer local market. Also the average transport cost per quintal is highest for large farms. The average distance to market is around 10 km.

Table 3.15

Distance and Type of Market

Factors	*Marginal*	*Small*	*Medium*	*Large*	*All Farms*
Sale in local market (HH%)	0.83	4.41	31.13	22.31	58.68*
Sell in distant market (HH%)	0.55	3.03	19.01	16.80	39.39*
Average transport cost (₹/qtl)	10.00	13.23	16.76	17.20	16.58
Average distance to market kms	10.40	5.07	10.21	11.70	10.42

Note: Since not all household belong to this category, it does not sum to hundred.

3.2.2 Policy Awareness

Generally less than a quarter of farmers are aware about policies like MSP (minimum support price) as a policy variable. One-sixth feel that sale possibilities can be availed and farmers feel that this is possible by retaining less for feed and around a tenth are aware of the possibilities of futures trading.

3.2.3 Credit

The institutional sources of credit are more dominant like banks and cooperative societies. Half of the medium farms and three quarters of large farms have access to credit. In our sample, the advantage of cooperative credit is largely taken by medium and large farms. The average amount of loan is around ₹ 1.5 lakh. Getting a loan from bank is not difficult. Table 3.17 summaries the sources of credit to farmers.

Table 3.16

Policy Awareness

Policy Categories	*Marginal*	*Small*	*Medium*	*Large*	*All Farms*
Aware of MSP (%)	0.00	11.11	20.77	31.25	23.96
Aware of Futures Trading (%)	0.00	25.93	7.65	13.19	11.14
Additional Sale Possibilities availed if available? Yes (%)	40.00	14.81	11.48	20.14	15.60
If Yes, Source					
a. Less Retention for seed	40.00	3.70	1.09	4.86	3.34
b. Less Retention for feed	0.00	11.11	7.10	10.42	8.64

Table 3.17

Sources of Credit by Farm Size

Factors Categories	*Marginal*	*Small*	*Medium*	*Large*	*All Farms*
Access to Credit (%)	20.00	14.81	53.55	77.78	59.89
Credit Sources:					
Private money lender	0.00	0.00	5.60	2.08	1.67
Relatives and Friends	0.00	0.00	1.64	0.69	1.11
Commercial Bank	0.00	11.11	31.15	56.94	39.55
Miller	0.00	0.00	0.00	0.00	0.00
Cooperative Society	20.00	3.70	19.13	18.06	17.55
Purpose:					
Average Loan Amount	25000	226250	94989.8	178866.1	140800
Problem in getting loan from bank (%)	0.00	0.00	1.67	2.23	3.90
Have Kisan Credit Card (KCC) (%)	0	0	10	19.44	12.81
Average KCC Limit	N.A.	N.A.	131333.3	315785.7	243608.7

Contract farming is rarely used (2-5% of farms, generally medium and large farms only.)

3.2.4 Sources of Price Information

The medium and large farmers are more networked, communication helps them more (Table 3.18).

By and large, the trader himself helps as a source of information though media is also availed.

Table 3.18

Sources of Price Information

(In Percentage)

Source of Price Information	*Marginal*	*Small*	*Medium*	*Large*	*All Farms*
Trader	40.00	55.56	75.96	72.92	72.70
Print media	0.00	22.22	46.45	62.50	50.42
Electronic media	0.00	7.41	7.10	12.50	9.19
Visit to Market	0.00	25.93	11.48	3.47	9.19
Others	0.00	18.52	4.37	4.86	5.57

3.3 Estimation of Marketed and Marketable Surplus and Comparison with Previous Studies

Surplus tends to be highest for wheat followed by *bajra* then oil seeds. This seems to result from the fact that wheat and *bajra* has more significant production (Table 3.19). For wheat around 73% of the availability is marketed (marketed surplus ratio) and our estimate is that around same is marketable (marketable surplus ratio). For *bajra,* these ratios are 71 per cent and 64 per cent and for oil seeds, the number is a little less than 70. A district-wise statistics for marketed to Marketable Surplus is shown in Table 3.20.

Table 3.19

Marketed and Marketable Surplus Ratio Estimates for Major Crops

Crop	*Marketed Surplus Ratio*	*Marketable Surplus Ratio*
Tur	69.54	69.40
Bajra	71.41	63.75
Wheat	73.89	73.88

Table 3.20

District-wise Marketed and Marketable Surplus Ratio Estimates for Crop

Districts	*Marketable Surplus Ratio*	*Marketed Surplus Ratio*
	Tur	
Baroda	70.42	70.26
Panchmahal	68.22	68.09
Overall	69.54	69.40
	Wheat	
Junagadh	81.51	81.51
Kheda	66.46	66.46
Banaskantha	37.17	37.14
Overall	73.89	73.88
	Bajra	
Kheda	73.95	73.94
Banaskantha	68.64	68.61
Overall	71.41	63.75

The exceptional values are seen in wheat, in Junagadh (high proportion marketed) and Banaskantha (low proportion marketed).

Table 3.21

Marketed and Marketable Surplus Ratio Estimates by Size Class

Land Size	*Marketable Surplus Ratio*	*Marketed Surplus Ratio*
	Tur	
Marginal	76.24	76.24
Small	47.46	47.46
Medium	76.53	76.43
Large	68.32	68.13
Overall	69.54	69.40
	Wheat	
Marginal	0.00	0.00
Small	12.93	12.93
Medium	67.36	67.36
Large	77.11	77.11
Overall	73.89	73.88
	Bajra	
Marginal	0.00	0.00
Small	43.82	43.79
Medium	66.47	66.44
Large	76.40	76.38
Overall	71.41	63.75

It cannot be concluded that surplus increases with size. A clear relationship is not seen. For small farms, a low value is seen (Table 3.21).

3.3.1 Comparison with Previous Studies

It would be interesting to see whether or not earlier studies (conducted in the late 1990s or even before the 1970s) would have different results i.e., a lower marketed surplus ratio for food grains like wheat and *bajra*. We find that this is indeed the case; the onset of liberalisation may not have led to greater emphasis on agriculture but has definitely led to a greater emphasis on the market as our results show.

The Directorate of Marketing & Inspection (DMI), ever since its inception in the year 1935, has been engaged in conducting surveys on marketing of agricultural commodities. In the recent past, a nationwide survey was conducted for estimation of marketable surplus and post-harvest losses of food grains on paddy, wheat, *jowar*, *bajra*, maize, ragi, barley amongst cereals and *arhar*, green gram, black gram, gram and lentil amongst pulses for the period of three years i.e., 1996-97, 1997-98 and 1998-99. The study covered 25 states, 100 selected districts and 15,000 cultivator households in the country with stratified multi-stage random sampling design. The survey generated valuable information on various aspects such as retention for different purpose, marketed surplus and marketable surplus, post-harvest losses at producer's level. We summarise below the results for wheat and *bajra* to compare with our study.

Wheat

1. The survey covered 100 districts, selected from 25 states, in accordance with the methodology approved by the Technical Committee, in consultation with the Indian Agriculture Statistical Research Institute (IASRI), New Delhi. From 100 selected districts, 1,500 villages were selected. Out of 1,500 selected villages, 1,065 selected villages were growing wheat. In other words, 71 per cent of the selected villages were wheat-growing villages.

2. The total area under wheat was estimated at 26,569.29 thousand ha. Out of this, an average of 22,859.40 ha or nearly 86.04 per cent was grown as irrigated.
3. The coverage of the high yielding varieties (HYVs) was of the order of 23,198.65 ha or 87.31 per cent.
4. The production of wheat was estimated at 68,495.89 tonnes; out of which, the contribution of irrigated wheat was 63,472.64 tonnes or 92.67 per cent. The contribution of HYVs in production was estimated at 62,778.63 tonnes or 91.65 per cent.
5. The total requirement of wheat for farm-family consumption (retention for consumption at farmer level and purchases) was estimated at 20,313.12 tonnes, which accounted for 29.66 per cent of the estimated production.
6. The total post-harvest losses of wheat at producers' level (in transport from field to threshing floor, threshing and winnowing, transportation and farm storage) were estimated at 1.79 per cent of the total production.
7. The total marketed surplus was estimated to be 53.81 per cent. The share of direct sales by the producers to consumers was 14.56 per cent. The cooperatives purchased only 9.42 per cent. The share of FCI was merely 20.00 per cent
8. Out of the total sales, 70.73 per cent sales were within villages.
9. The earlier survey of marketable surplus and post-harvest losses of wheat conducted during the year 1972-73 revealed that estimated farm-family requirement was 7,525.83 tonnes or 34.92 per cent of estimated production. Incidentally, it may be mentioned that during the year, the country was facing the problem of deficit.
10. The 1972-73 survey showed that the marketable surplus was 14,028.57 tonnes or 65.08 per cent of the production. The present survey revealed that the marketable surplus now stood at 39,288.34 tonnes or 57.36 per cent and the total farm-family requirement including the losses at farm level accounted for 29207.55 tonnes or 42.64 per cent of the total production.

11. The 1970s surveys showed that the average number of family members per household was 6.26, whereas the 1970s survey showed that the average number of family members per household was 6.45.

Bajra

1. The survey covered 100 districts selected from 25 states in accordance with the methodology approved by the Technical Committee in consultation with the IASRI, New Delhi. From 100 selected districts, 1,500 villages were selected. Out of 1,500 selected villages, 313 villages were growing *bajra*. In other words, 20.87 of the selected villages were *bajra*-growing villages.
2. The total area under *bajra* was estimated at 9,761.44 ha. Out of this, an average of 2787.59 thousand hectares or nearly 28.56 per cent was grown as irrigated. The state-wise distribution of area under *bajra* showed that maximum area was in the state of Rajasthan (4,700.00 ha), followed by Maharashtra (1,750.01 ha), Gujarat (1,075.00 ha), Uttar Pradesh (850.00 ha), Haryana (574.97 ha), Karnataka (350.00 ha), Tamil Nadu (189.98 ha) and Madhya Pradesh (140.00 ha). These states together accounted for 99.69 per cent of area under *bajra*. Rajasthan had highest per cent irrigated area i.e., 51.23 per cent.
3. The coverage of the HYVs was of the order of 7,404.58 ha or 75.86 per cent.
4. The production of *bajra* was estimated at 7,948.85 tonnes, out of which the contribution of irrigated *bajra* was 2,760.47 ha or 34.73 per cent. The contribution of HYVs in production was estimated at 6,475.78 tonnes or 81.47 per cent. This further signifies the need for promotion of HYV.
5. The total requirement of *bajra* for farm-family consumption (retention for consumption at farmer level and purchases) was estimated at 2,854.64 tonnes, which accounted for 35.91 per cent of the estimated production.

6. The estimates of retention for various purposes and purchases of *bajra* to meet the total requirement of farm-family were as follows:

i)	For farm-family consumption	-	34.80 per cent
ii)	For consumption by permanent labour and temporary labour	-	1.11 per cent
iii)	Estimated purchases for consumption	-	0.02 per cent
iv)	For seed purpose	-	0.49 per cent
v)	For animal feed	-	4.90 per cent
vi)	For payment in cash and kind	-	1.19 per cent

7. The total post-harvest losses of *bajra* at producers' level (in transport from field to threshing floor, threshing and winnowing, transportation and farm storage) were estimated at 1.89 per cent of the total production.
8. The total marketed surplus was estimated to be 45.44 per cent. In the total sale, the share of direct sales by the producers to consumers was 10.80 per cent. The cooperatives purchased only 5.92 per cent. The share of FCI was merely 0.38 per cent.
9. Out of the total sales, 43.45 per cent sales were within villages.
10. The earlier survey of marketable surplus and post-harvest losses of *Bajra* conducted during the year 1974-75 revealed that estimated farm-family requirement was 1,994.45 tonnes or 63.69 per cent of estimated production.
11. The 1974-75 survey showed that the marketable surplus was 1,137.15 tonnes or 36.31 per cent of the production. The present survey revealed that the marketable surplus now stood at 3,893.61 tonnes or 48.98 per cent and the total farm-family requirement including the losses at farm level accounted for 4,055.24 tonnes or 51.02 per cent of the total production.
12. The marketed surplus was estimated at 3,612.11 tonnes i.e., 45.44 per cent of total production.

13. The 1990s survey showed that the farm-family requirement was 4,055.24 tonnes. During the 1974-75 survey, it was observed to be 1,994.45 tonnes. Thus, farm-family requirement seemed to have increased by 103 per cent.
14. The 1970s surveys showed that the average number of family members per household was 6.26, whereas the 1990s survey showed that the average number of family members per household was 6.45.

3.4 Regression Relating Factors Affecting Marketed Surplus

We are interested in estimating the determination of marketed surplus ratio of total crops to related variables as described in the methodology chapter and on the basis of our quantitative results.

MS (Y) = f [farm-size (X1), household size (X2),access to credit (X3), off farm income (X4), distance from market (X5), age (X6), expense on tube wells (X7), no. of tractors (X8), number of tube wells (X9), number of cattle (X10), awareness of MSP (X11), education of the decision maker in years(X12), belonging to general caste (X13), sale price (X14)]

Here, the independent variable Y is the marketed surplus of individual farms aggregated and the independent variables are as stated. It is important to note that variables like years of education and access to credit do not show relationship with marketed surplus. It should be noted here that as some of the farm households do not actually market their product (the entire product is retained for home consumption), we have intentionally left them out from our exercise. Out of the total of 360 farm households covered under the study, we included only farm households who have marketed at least some part of their product. The result of the regression exercise stated above is presented in Tables 3.22, 3.23 and 3.24 for oil seeds, wheat and *bajra* respectively. From the results of our regression exercise, it is seen that the regression coefficients are highly significant. The exercise reveals that factors representing developed agriculture, have a significant positive effect on marketed surplus ratio, which means that more modern the agriculture more it induces them to sell proportionate higher amounts of crop in the market. Modern technology in agriculture leads to larger surpluses to sell.

Table 3.22

Regression Values of Factors Affecting Marketed Surplus of Tur in Gujarat (2011-12)

Factors	*Coefficient*	*Std. Error*	*t-ratio*	*p-value*	
Constant	564.378	733.385	0.7696	0.44550	
Area in hectare	20.3569	16.418	1.2399	0.22130	
Family size	-88.8842	40.6251	-2.1879	0.03379	**
Access to credit	732.958	317.871	2.3058	0.02568	**
Education in years	127.191	33.7097	3.7731	0.00046	***
Price sold in ₹	-0.0755889	0.164695	-0.4590	0.64842	
No. of tube wells	100.591	256.256	0.3925	0.69647	
No. of tractors	750.269	264.761	2.8338	0.00681	***
No. of cattle	172.139	54.183	3.1770	0.00266	***
Belonging to general caste	-879.013	369.096	-2.3815	0.02143	**
Statistics based on the weighted data:					
Sum squared residual	141.7827	S.E. of regression	1.755629		
R-squared	0.920341	Adjusted R-squared	0.903023		
F(10, 46)	53.14592	P-value(F)	6.84e-22		
Log-likelihood	-106.8500	Akaike criterion	235.6999		
Schwarz criterion	258.1735	Hannan-Quinn	244.4339		
Statistics based on the original data:					
Mean dependent variable	1493.737	S.D. dependent variable	2161.380		
Sum squared residual	2.19e+08	S.E. of regression	2182.675		

Note: ** and *** denote significance at 0.01 and 0.001 levels respectively.
Regression is heteroskedasticity-corrected, using observations 1-57.
Dependent variable: marketed surplus.

Tur surpluses are negatively related with family size on account of self-consumption. Educated upper caste farmers have larger surpluses to sell. Investment variables have a positive relationship with marketed surpluses. The F value of 53.15 is significantly higher than the required value of 2.66 for 10.46 degrees of freedom at 1 per cent level leading to highly significant estimated relationship.

Table 3.23

Regression Values of Factors Affecting Marketed Surplus of Wheat in Gujarat (2011-12)

Factors	*Coefficient*	*Std. Error*	*t-ratio*	*p-value*	
Constant	-1415.01	1828.56	-0.7738	0.44246	
Area in hectare	82.218	29.2502	2.8109	0.00691	***
Access to credit	90.1533	578.33	0.1559	0.87672	
Family size	-266.4	91.6891	-2.9055	0.00534	***
Off farm income	0.00707131	0.00580922	1.2173	0.22890	
Price sold in ₹	2.0129	1.09883	1.8319	0.07259	*
Dummy mkt. distant/local (positive sign because if farmer sells in distant market rather than disposing off product in local market itself means higher marketed amount is there)	746.882	364.452	2.0493	0.04539	**
Aware of MSP	49.4238	872.628	0.0566	0.95505	
No. of tractors	513.805	415.804	1.2357	0.22202	
No. of tube wells	1372.73	359.548	3.8179	0.00035	***
Age in years	5.39637	16.2133	0.3328	0.74057	
Belonging to general caste	-51.1739	453.248	-0.1129	0.91053	
Cattle	-479.297	206.017	-2.3265	0.02385	**
Education in years	108.687	55.9571	1.9423	0.05742	*
Statistics based on the weighted data:					
Sum squared residual	195.5214	S.E. of regression	1.920699		
R-squared	0.737221	Adjusted R-squared	0.672765		
F(13, 53)	11.43770	P-value(F)	3.67e-11		
Log-likelihood	-130.9466	Akaike criterion	289.8932		
Schwarz criterion	320.7589	Hannan-Quinn	302.1069		
Statistics based on the original data:					
Mean dependent variable	2746.672		S.D. dependent variable	3596.751	
Sum squared residual	4.84e+08		S.E. of regression	3022.581	

Note: *, ** and *** denote significance at 0.05, 0.01 and 0.001 levels respectively.
Regression is heteroskedasticity-corrected, using observations 1-67.
Dependent variable: marketed surplus.

The relationship is again highly significant. The required F value at 1 per cent level for 13.53 degrees of freedom is 2.45 and the estimated level is 11.44. Higher family size means lower surplus on account of self-consumption. A better price and sale at the distant market lead to higher surpluses. Investment variables like tube wells, farm size and the number of cattle are significant as well as education levels.

Table 3.24

Regression Values of Factors Affecting Marketed Surplus of Bajra in Gujarat 2011-12

Factors	*Coefficient*	*Std. Error*	*t-ratio*	*p-value*	
Constant	-1078.43	985.052	-1.0948	0.27621	
Area in hectare	330.351	57.1952	5.7759	<0.00001	***
Off farm income	0.00778132	0.0035136	2.2146	0.02903	**
Dummy Market distant/local	2468.04	751.284	3.2851	0.00140	***
Price sold in ₹	1.66534	0.445309	3.7397	0.00031	***
Aware of MSP	1965.87	956.745	2.0547	0.04249	**
Age in years	-18.4165	15.7928	-1.1661	0.24631	
Number of tube wells	194.597	376.985	0.5162	0.60685	
Number of tractors	1809.24	522.192	3.4647	0.00078	***
Statistics based on the weighted data:					
Sum squared residual	241.8645	S.E. of regression	1.547481		
R-squared	0.572029	Adjusted R-squared	0.521181		
F(12, 101)	11.24979	P-value(F)	5.85e-14		
Log-likelihood	-204.6332	Akaike criterion	435.2664		
Schwarz criterion	470.8370	Hannan-Quinn	449.7025		
Statistics based on the original data:					
Mean dependent variable	4034.004	S.D. dependent variable	6084.049		
Sum squared residual	2.22e+09	S.E. of regression	4689.296		

Note: *, ** and *** denote significance at 0.05, 0.01 and 0.001 levels respectively.
Regression is heteroskedasticity-corrected, using observations 1-114.
Dependent variable: marketed surplus.

Bajra in this result is more like a commercial crop. Self-consumption in terms of family size is not significant. The price obtained is important as also sale in the distant market. The study finds that in *bajra* there is a preponderance of large farmers, having non-farm income, aware of the MSP for *bajra* and investing in farm machinery.

4

Summary and Conclusion

4.1 Need of the Study

Gujarati farmers have increased in prosperity with Sardar Sarovar, however certain traits remain: they insure a certain amount of grain for self-consumption, around 30 per cent at all times. There are certain basic features of the system and environment which affect this propensity of self-consumption: storage facilities are limited, irrigation till recently was by digging borewells and electric tube wells, canal irrigation through Sardar Sarovar has led to demand for electricity for irrigation declining. Specifically as far as the impact of irrigation on the farmers is concerned, we can say that large farmers having some ability to ensure storage of water in Kheda and Vadodara falling in catchment areas of Sardar Sarovar have become more prosperous. The situation of small farmers has also improved due to excess flood waters and catchment area of Mahi Canal in these two districts. As far as the rest of the study area is concerned in Saurashtra and rocky areas of Panchmahal, the impact of Narmada is not yet felt. So we cannot say actual impact of Narmada project has begun to be felt in substantial pockets of the sample area covered. Despite increasing prosperity a certain minimum percentage of the crop is still retained, specifically with regard to food grains. However all the above is based on observation and study of agriculture in Gujarat, a definite conclusion could have only emerged through a detailed statistical field study which we attempted as above was the basic path taken in the study and conclusions reached.

4.2 Objectives of the Study

The main objectives of the study were to estimate marketable and marketed surplus of selected food grains in Gujarat and to examine the role of institutional, infrastructural and socioeconomic factors in influencing household marketed surplus decisions.

Wheat, *bajra* and *tur* are the largest food grain crops in Gujarat. The study covered five districts: Vadodara, Panchmahal, Kheda, Junagadh and Banaskantha. The crops covered were *tur* in Vadodara and Panchmahal, wheat and *bajra* in Kheda, wheat in Junagadh and *bajra* in Banaskantha. The production of these crops specially in these districts were dominant in Gujarat. Totally 359 respondents were interviewed: 50 each in Vadodara and Panchmahal, 101 in Kheda, 80 in Junagadh and 78 in Banaskantha.

Sample size was selected for each district. Village level detailed farming information relevant for estimating marketed surplus was obtained from the field survey at the village level. This included: sale price, productivity, machinery used, cropping pattern, irrigation mechanisms and so on. During these visits, project head visited the villages along with field staff at the first instance to create suitable rapport with the villagers. This was followed in every village by detailed surveying by the field investigators, supervised by the author as project incharge.

4.3 The Growth Performance for Major Crops in Gujarat

The growth performance for major crops reveals that the post-liberalisation phase was marked by improvements in yield levels for all the major food crops, groundnut and cotton. Food grains as a category recorded a decline in acreage up to 2000-01. Between 2001 and 2010, the share of food grain area in gross cropped area (GCA) stabilised at around 34 per cent. While *bajra*, *jowar* and maize recorded a decline in acreage growth, wheat area expanded very rapidly (estimated to be 10.7% annually) that arrested the falling importance of food grains in the agricultural economy of the state. Commercialisation process and crop diversification towards non-food crops (cotton, spices, horticulture) are positive developments. Castor and sesame besides groundnut are the other commercial crops that are amenable to processing and have expanding domestic and global demand (Mehta, 2012a)

4.4 Summary of Performance of Top Performing Districts Including Selected Districts in Selected Crops

4.4.1 Characteristics of Sampled Population

Average age of the decision makers of the sample households is near 50, therefore like in census households, here too middle aged farmers predominate. Possibly younger members are migrating out. Farm households have larger family size as compared to census results. The fact that farm household size is more than 4-5 persons as in the census implies that family is not nuclear but is larger. The average size is 6.7. The size of households of marginal and large farms is above 7. Large farmers can support a large family size. Marginal farmers have a low land base but the family members are forced to depend on agriculture. The main occupation is crop farming in all farm sizes and dairying dominates as a subsidiary occupation. Dairying is a subsidiary and important occupation in rural India now and this is particularly true for Gujarat. In terms of caste composition general category predominates, followed by OBC (other backward class) and then SC (schedule caste). In fact the general category proportion is much higher in large farms which would imply operational ownership of landed property by the upper castes in most prosperous tracts in Gujarat, though this requires further detailed study to confirm the phenomena as also the hypothesis resulting from that. Generally medium and large farmers tend to dominate in all classifications. This is particularly so since they have leased in irrigated land in what we described as reverse tenancy.

4.4.2 Area

In terms of percentage of GCA, cotton is a major crop, so is wheat. Paddy and vegetables are grown in the *kharif* season. Area is also being allocated to other crops like tobacco and potato; this proportion is greater than cotton. As far as *rabi* season is concerned wheat is grown on 25% of the land. This is traditionally an area where paddy and wheat farming was giving way to oil seeds and commercial crops. Sardar Sarovar Project (SSP) seems to have made the return to paddy and wheat. At the present stage, SSP waters are uncontrolled at the delivery level and flood irrigation leads to paddy and wheat farming predominating. Cotton farming, as we saw in the earlier sections, has been very successful in fields of Gujarat on account of the new Bt technology and it has spearheaded Gujarat's agricultural growth in the last decade and a half. Oil seeds, cotton, vegetables and fruits are all grown largely in medium and large farms. Commercialisation is therefore more in such farms.

4.4.3 Production

Output outcomes follow from area allocations, particularly of irrigated area. Sardar Sarovar canal irrigation has also led to a resurgence of *kharif* paddy. The proportion follows from area with other crops, *kharif* cotton, paddy, oil seeds and pulses production in that order. As it is obvious, the production of *rabi* wheat is high. Major output consequences are in medium and large farms; taking the agricultural year as a whole, wheat emerges in quantity terms as the largest crop. This is noteworthy because cereals were falling as a proportion of Gujarat agriculture in earlier decades. SSP has led to this reversal. Another noteworthy crop is cotton, in which the performance is driven by technology. The falling importance of oil seeds comes out. The medium and large farmers are the main actors in Gujarat's agricultural performance. For example, as compared to 0.81 ha under cotton for small farms, the figure for medium farms is 39.04 ha and that for large farms is 185.85 ha. Again in our sample, vegetables are grown in medium and large farms.

4.4.4 Yield

Generally across farm size categories, yield tends to not fluctuate too much. It is interesting that the relation between farm size and productivity still shows that in some crops small farms hold out in their performance. This aspect will be studied more in the econometric analysis of this study.

4.4.5 Source of Irrigation

Electric tube wells are the major source of irrigation; in some areas, irrigation is done by diesel tube wells and bore wells as well. This shows that there is sufficient supply of electricity for irrigation. Our sample shows that investment in tube wells is high. There is a great thrust for water in Gujarat agriculture and this continues with SSP water. There are many areas of over-exploitation and are called 'grey areas' in our sample areas. Since SSP water supply is not controlled, paddy cultivation is done with canal water. Paddy cultivation can be done with flood irrigation.

4.4.6 Farm Machinery

Use of farm machines is constrained by considerations of profitability. A large amount of expenditure on tractors, tube wells and threshing machines was seen by farmers in these areas, indicating prosperity. High expense on an average on tractors and tube wells is seen, indicating sufficient purchase and use by medium and large farmers.

4.4.7 Livestock

Maintaining cattle/buffalo is not a viable proposition for the smaller farms, as their use has become extremely confined in the face of competition from tractors under modern cultivation practices. Livestock and fodder prices are also inflating.

Across all size classes, livestock other than cattle/buffalo is not kept, as the average number of ruminants is quite low which confirms their prohibitive costs.

Across farm sizes, apart from small farms, farmer households have large per hectare cattle holding since dairying is a major source of livelihood. Of course, medium and large farms have larger herd size. Small farms maintain much larger herd size in relation to their land holding. Livestock per household in large farms is very high; this is a feature which results naturally in societies where number of cattle owned is seen as a sign of wealth.

4.4.8 Sale Price

Pulses have a sale price of above 3,200/qtl except small farms which is lower than 3,000/qtl. Oil seeds also have the same range of sale price/qtl, with small farmers selling at 3,000/qtl. Cotton across farm size sells at above 3,700/qtl. Vegetables sell for about ten times as much though there is variation in the price across and within size classes. *Kharif* paddy sells for around ₹ 1000/qtl. *Rabi* wheat sells for more than ₹ 1000/qtl. Small farmers get lower prices around 10-25 per cent lower than large. There are exceptions in data like in vegetables where medium farmers seem to be growing higher value added vegetables and large farmers growing is low value added vegetables. The major feature which emerge is the better terms received in the market by medium and large farmers. The impression that in Gujarat cooperative institutions lead to improved terms for small and marginal farms is not borne out by this study.

4.4.9 Production and Availability of Crop by Farm Size

For all crops there is hardly any beginning stock per household at an average, the larger two farm sizes have higher average production in the season, i.e. large farmers produce more. Production clearly rises with farm size. In *tur*, medium farmer household grow 9.41 qtl per household and large farmer households grow 16.73 qtl. In wheat, these figures are 24.04 qtl and 76.12 qtl respectively. *Bajra* is grown by marginal farms but only 9.46 qtl per household. The numbers for small households are slightly higher at 11.76 qtl but those of medium farms are 27.78 qtl and of large farm households 81.41 qtl.

4.4.10 Sale Pattern of Selected Crops

Average sale is approximately 7 qlt for *tur*, 46 qtl for wheat and 40 qtl for *bajra*. *Tur* sales are 1 to approximately 2 qtl per farm for marginal and small farms. These are 4.09 and 10.85 for medium and large farm households. In wheat, the differences are more. Small farms sell 3.6 qtl per household, but medium farms sell 22.85 qtl and large farm households sell 73.47 qtl.

Sales are generally to private trader/money lender and increase monotonically by size. Average price received per quintal by private trader is ₹ 2500-3500 in *tur*, around ₹ 1100 in wheat and ₹ 800-980 in *bajra*. The processor or millers and private companies work on a commission basis in processing *dals*.

4.4.11 Crop Retention Pattern

Generally retention rises with farm size. In the case of *tur* retention of marginal and small farmers is around a third of large farmer households. Medium farmers also have a slightly higher retention than marginal and small farms. *Tur dal* is an item of consumption and probably has a high income elasticity of demand. Large farm households also purchase *tur dal* to a much larger extent. For all crops across farm size categories of farmers, retention for self-consumption goes up with farm size. Small farms tend to purchase more.

4.4.12 Crop Losses

Crop losses are generally attained during harvesting. Interestingly, small farmers have a significant proportion of losses. It should also be mentioned here that crop loss in harvesting depends much upon factors like the state of maturity of crops, timing of harvesting, unwanted rainfall in the maturity period, distance of plot from farmhouse, etc. This study does not take into account of such factors separately and provides the overall estimate of crop loss during harvesting.

4.4.13 Crop Losses during Transport

Transport losses from field to floor and floor to market are attained basically while transporting through tractor. Crop losses occur during transport of crop output. This happens mainly during transporting harvested crop from field to threshing floor and transporting stored crop from farm to market.

Losses are generally attained while transporting through tractor that being the dominant mode of transportation. Some losses are also attained while transporting by person on head, as well as by animal. Losses in packing are during packing in bags.

4.5 Factors Influencing Marketed Surplus

4.5.1 Distance and Type of Market

A greater proportion (60%) of farmers sell in local market across farm sizes. However around 40 per cent of households sell in distant markets. The farmer generally prefers local market. Also the average transport cost per quintal is highest for large farms. The average distance to market is around 10 kms.

4.5.2 Policy Awareness

Generally, less than a quarter of farmers are aware about policies like MSP (minimum support price) as a policy variable. One-sixth feel that sale possibilities can be availed; and farmers feel that this is possible by retaining less for feed. Around a tenth are aware of the possibilities of futures trading.

4.5.3 Credit

Generally larger farmers are aware about credit. The institutional sources of credit are more dominant like banks and cooperative societies. Half of the medium farms and three quarters of large farms have access to credit. The average amount of loan is around ₹ 1.5 lakh. Getting a loan from bank is not difficult.

4.5.4 Contract Farming

Contract farming is rarely used (2-5% of farms, generally medium and large farms only).

4.5.5 Sources of Price Information

The medium and large farmers are more networked, communication helps them more. By and large, the trader acts as a source of information, though media is also available.

4.6 Estimation of Marketed and Marketable Surplus

Surplus tends to be highest for wheat followed by *bajra* then *tur*; this seems to result from the fact that wheat and *bajra* have more significant production. For wheat, around 73 per cent of the availability is marketed (marketed surplus ratio) and our estimate is that around same is marketable (marketable surplus ratio). For *bajra,* these ratios are 71 per cent and 64 per cent and for *tur* the number is a little less than 70.

The exceptional values are seen in wheat, in Junagadh (high proportion marketed) and Banaskantha (low proportion marketed). It cannot be concluded that surplus increases with size. A clear relationship is not seen. For small farms, a low value is seen. Quantitatively wheat and *bajra* have a larger marketed surplus.

Quantitatively since more than a fifth of the area (GCA) is allocated to wheat, its predominance in quantities is obvious. Of course given the size and purposive nature of the sample, these estimates are of an indicative nature.

4.7 Regression Relating Factors Affecting Marketed Surplus with Marketed Surplus Value

Regression exercises reveal that factors representing developed agriculture have a significant positive effect on marketed surplus ratio, which means that the more modern the agriculture, more it induces them to sell proportionate higher amounts of crop in the market. Investments in tube wells and farm machinery are significant variables determining surplus. These would be farms taking advantage of modern technology in agriculture and have larger surpluses to sell. Larger farms have more surpluses. Self-consumption is important in *tur* and wheat as shown in relation with family size. Interestingly, *bajra* shows the character of a commercial crop with the surplus related with price, distance to market and non-farm income.

4.8 Concluding Observations and Policy Implications

The present study is undertaken with the objective of estimation of marketed and marketable surplus at producer's level for *tur*, *bajra* and wheat, the important food grain crops of Gujarat. The study is based on primary data from 359 households spread over five districts of Gujarat. The primary data pertain to the year 2011-12.

4.8.1 Production

Major output consequences are in medium and large farms, taking the agricultural year as a whole; wheat emerges in quantity terms as the largest crop. This is noteworthy because cereals were falling as a proportion of Gujarat agriculture in earlier decades. SSP has led to this reversal. The medium and large farmers are the main actors in Gujarat's agricultural performance.

The major feature which emerges is the better terms received in the market by medium and large farmers. The impression that in Gujarat cooperative institutions lead to improved terms for small and marginal farms is not borne out by this study. Our sample shows that investment in tube wells is high. There is a great thrust for water in Gujarat agriculture and this continues with SSP water. Use of farm machines is constrained by considerations of profitability; a large amount of expenditure on tractors, tube wells and threshing machines was seen by farmers in these areas, indicating prosperity. Maintaining cattle/buffalo is not a viable proposition for the smaller farms, as their use has become extremely confined in the face of competition from tractors under modern cultivation practices. Sales are generally to private trader/money lender and increase monotonically by size. Generally retention rises with farm size. Crop losses are generally attained during harvesting. It should also be mentioned here that crop loss in harvesting depends much upon factors like the state of maturity of crops, timing of harvesting, unwanted rainfall in the maturity period, distance of plot from farmhouse, etc. Majority of the larger farmers are aware about credit. The institutional sources of credit are more dominant like banks and cooperative societies.

4.8.2 Market Information

The medium and large farmers are more networked, communication helps them more. By and large, the trader acts as a source of information, though other media is also available.

4.8.3 Regression Relating Factors Affecting Marketed Surplus with Marketed Surplus Value

The exercise reveals that factors representing developed agriculture have a significant positive effect on marketed surplus ratio, which means that, more modern the agriculture, more it induces them to sell proportionate higher amounts of crop in the market.

4.8.4 Policy Implications

Development of efficient agricultural marketing is crucial for accelerating the growth of agricultural production and marketed surplus. An efficient marketing system must ensure best possible return for sale of produce. The investigation reveals that food grains market is highly dominated by private sector and traders were observed to exploit producers in the absence of an organised dissemination of market information.

The study reveals that majority households were lacking marketing intelligence. Majority of households were receiving information from traders regarding the market.

The study illustrated that total production losses at different stages of handling were high. By minimising the losses at different stages, marketed surplus and financial benefits to producers can be enhanced. For minimisation of losses, technical backup and support with regard to scientific storage, use of mechanical operations at harvesting stages, and mode of packing and transportation should be disseminated. Moreover, creation of proper and adequate storage facilities at producers' level will reduce the storage losses and enhance the bargaining power of producers in the marketing of produce, which will create positive impact on their net profitability.

The study revealed that marketed surplus output ratio was found on the lower side because the farmer always insures minimum amount of (approximately 30%) output for self-consumption.

The study revealed marketed surplus of all four crops are lower than marketable surplus. In Gujarat, distress sales is anyway not much seen.

The study gives clear message that if storage, seeds and pest removal is stepped up and the farmer is given even greater support by more enthusiastic government machinery and officers, the food security of the farmers can increase. This is the only way the retention proportion of Gujarati farmers can be reduced, but this is a slow process, it will take decades not years. Further work from this study could involve estimating a production function determined by commercialisation and market linkages and networking including modern inputs and credit which this study shows is seen to operate in Gujarat.

References

Acharya, Shankar (2011). "Agriculture: Be Like Gujarat: Other States have much to Learn from Indian Agriculture's Star Performer", *Business Standard*, 14 July.

Acharya, S.S. and N.L. Agarwal (2010). *Agricultural Marketing in India*. Oxford and IBH.

Ahmed, A. and V.P.S. Arora (1990). "A Study on Marketed Surplus and its Farm Level Determinant of Paddy in Assam", *Agricultural Marketing* 33(2).

Bardhan, K. (1970). "Price and Output Response of Marketed Surplus of Food Grains: A Cross-Sectional Study of Some North Indian Villages", *American Journal of Agricultural Economics* LII(1): 51-61, February.

Bardhan, P. and K. Bardhan (1971). "Price Response of Marketed Surplus of Food Grains: An Analysis of Indian Time-Series Data", *Oxford Economic Papers, New Series* XXIII(2): 255-67, July.

Behrman, J.R. (1966). "Price Elasticity of the Marketed Surplus of a Subsistence Crop", *Journal of Farm Economics* XLVIII(4): 875-93, November, Part 1.

Chand, R. (1991). *Agricultural Development Price Policy and Marketed Surplus in India Study of Green Revolution Region*. New Delhi: Concept.

Chattopadhyay, M. and I. Sen (1988). "Marketable Surplus and Size-Classes of Holdings", *Economic and Political Weekly* XXIII(52-53): A151-A156, 24-31 December.

Childs, D. and M. Kidron (1975). "Measuring the Surplus in India: Sources and Methods", *Economic and Political Weekly* X(9): 399-416, 1 March.

Dholakia, Ravindra (2007). "Sources of Economic Growth and Acceleration in Gujarat", *Economic and Political Weekly* XLII(9): 770-78, 3 March.

————. (2010). "Has Agriculture in Gujarat Shifted to High Growth Path?", Ravindra Dholakia and Samar K. Datta, *High Growth Trajectory and Structural Changes in Gujarat Agriculture*. Ahmedabad: Indian Institute of Management.

————. (2014). "Relative Growth Performance of Gujarat", *Economic & Political Weekly* 49(18): 75.

Dholakia, Ravindra and Samar Datta (2010). *High Growth Trajectory and Structural Changes in Gujarat Agriculture*. Ahmedabad: Indian Institute of Management.

Dixit, Anita K. (2009). "Agriculture in a High Growth State: The Case of Gujarat 1960 to 2006", *Economic and Political Weekly* XLIV(50): 64-71, 12 December.

Dubey, V. (1963). "The Marketed Agricultural Surplus and Economic Growth in Underdeveloped Countries", *The Economic Journal* LXXIII(292): 689-702, December.

Edmeades, Svetlana, Melinda Smale, Mitch Renkow and Dan Phaneuf (2004). "Variety Demand within the Framework of an Agricultural Household Model with Attributes: The Case of Bananas in Uganda", *EPTD Discussion Paper* No.125. Washington: International Food Policy Research Institute (IFPRI).

Ghatak S. and K. Insergent (1984). *Agriculture and Economic Development*. New Delhi: Select.

Gulati, Ashok, Tushar Shah and Ganga Shreedhar (2009). *Agriculture Performance in Gujarat since 2000: Can it be a Divadandi (Lighthouse) for other States?* Washington, D.C.: International Water Management Institute Colombo/International Food Policy Research Institute. May.

Hati, A. (1976). "Non-Linear Marketable Surplus Functions", *Economic and Political Weekly* XI(29): 1080-84, 17 July.

Khatkhate, D.R. (1962). "Some Notes on the Real Effects of Foreign Surplus Disposal in Underdeveloped Economies", *The Quarterly Journal of Economics* LXXVI(2): 186-96, May.

Krishna, Raj (1967). "Agricultural Price Policy and Economic Development", in H.M. Southworth and B.F. Johnston (eds.), *Agricultural Development and Economic Growth.* pp.497-540.

————. (1962). "A Note on the Elasticity of the Marketable Surplus of a Subsistence Crop", *Indian Journal of Agricultural Economics* XVII: 79-84.

Krishnan, T. N. (1965). "The Marketed Surplus of Food grains : Is it Inversely Related to Price?", *The Economic Weekly* XVII(7): 325-28, 13 February.

Kumar, Dinesh M., A. Narayanamoorthy, O.P. Singh, M.V.K. Sivamohan, Manoj Sharma and Nitin Bassi (2010). "Gujarat's Agricultural Growth Story Exploding Some Myths", *Occasional Paper* No.2-0410. Hyderabad: Institute for Resource Analysis and Policy.

Lancaster, K. (1966). "A New Approach to Consumer Theory", *The Journal of Political Economy* LXXIV(2): 132-57, April

Mathur, P. N. and Ezekiel, H. (1961). "Marketable Surplus of Food and Price Fluctuations in a Developing Economy", *Kyklos* XIV: 396-408, August.

Medani, A.I. (1975). "Elasticity of the Marketable Surplus of a Subsistence Crop at Various Stages of Development", *Economic Development and Cultural Change* XXIII(3): 421-29, April.

Mehta, Niti (2012). "Performance of Crop Sector in Gujarat during High Growth Period: Some Explorations", *Agricultural Economics Research Review* XXV(2).

————. (2012b). *Identifying Features of High Agricultural Growth in Gujarat in the Recent Period.* Department of Economic Analysis and Research, NABARD. June.

Mundle, S. (1977). "Home Market, Capitalism in Agriculture, and Drain of Agricultural Surplus", *Economic and Political Weekly* XII(26): A49-A54, 25 June.

Narian, D. (1961). *Distribution of Marketed Surplus of Agricultural Produce by Size Level of Holding in India: 1950-51.* Bombay: Asia.

Newman, M.D. (1977). *Determinants of Marketed Surplus in Rural Households: Towards an Applied Research Agenda from an African Policy Perspective.* Michigan State University Research Monograph.

Parmod Kumar (1999), "Marketed Surplus of Different Crops across Farm Size: A Study in Haryana", *Indian Journal of Agricultural Economics* 54(4).

Pattnaik, Itishree, and Amita Shah (2013). "Gujarat's Agricultural Growth Model: How Sustainable it is", *International Journal of Agriculture and Food Science Technology* 4: 281-86.

Patnaik, U. (1975). "Contribution to the Output and Marketable Surplus of Agricultural Products by Cultivating Groups in India, 1960-61", *Economic and Political Weekly* X(52): A90-A93, A95-A97, A99-A100, 27 December.

Ramesh Chand (2016). "Farmer Needs a New Deal", *Indian Express*, 16 March.

Rangi, P.S. (1993), "Production and Marketing Problems of Rice in Punjab State", *Agricultural Marketing* 35(4).

Reddy, M.J. M. (1987). "Marketed Surplus in Paddy: A Regression Analysis", *Agricultural Situation in India* (January).

Sadhu, A.N. and Singh, A. (2000). *Fundamentals of Agricultural Economics.* Himalaya.

Shah, Tushaar, Ashok Gulati, P. Hemant, Sreedhar Ganga and R.C. Jain (2009). "Secret of Gujarat's Agrarian Miracle after 2000", *Economic and Political Weekly* XLIV(52): 45-55, 26 December.

Srinivasan, M. (1961). "Problems of Marketable Surplus in Indian Agriculture", *Indian Journal of Agricultural Economics* XVI(1), January-March.

Thamarajakshi, R. (1969). "Intersectoral Terms of Trade and Marketed Surplus of Agricultural Produce, 1951-52 to 1965-66", *Economic and Political Weekly* IV(26): A91-A102, 28 June.

Upender, M. and Ch. Thirupathi (1998), "Marketed Surplus of Paddy: A Study at Farm level", *The Bihar Journal of Agricultural Marketing* VI(3): 249-62.

Appendix

Efficiency of Inputs, Technological Backup and Networking in Gujarat Agriculture

A Presentation of the Marketed Surplus Book
by Munish Alagh for Academic Foundation at JNU on 16.03.2016.
Dr. Munish Alagh

Gujarati farmers like farmers all over the world retain a certain amount of the food-crop they always keep in store with themselves as a legitimate insurance to ensure that their families are fed in case of crop failure, this proportion of about 30% of the food crop is not going to change over the years irrespective of economic development, the farmer continues to be cautious.

Retention-Tur dal is an item of consumption and probably has a high income elasticity of demand. Certain amount of foodgrain is always retained for guarantee against crop failure.

Why do the farmers retain some amount of food crop instead of selling whole produce?

As an insurance against crop risk, they need to keep certain amount for Household Consumption. Sometimes despite their best effort they do not get real price expected in market, so they store for expectation of higher price in future.

Gujarati farmers studied in my report stated certain major problems, firstly at the basic farming stage Gujarati farmers stated a major problem with Pests. Pests like wild pig, donkeys and locusts in field and rats and insects at Storage Stage. Farmers state lack of knowledge of pesticides and measures to deal with pests as a major problem. Local tools which are used by neighbouring farms is copied, government help is requested to get rid of this scourge.

1. The study on "Assessment of Marketed and Marketable Surplus of Major Foodgrains in Gujarat" was sponsored by the Ministry of Agriculture, Government of India, New Delhi. The questions listed above were asked during personal interviews of 359 farmers in districts of Gujarat growing tur, bajra and Wheat. The responses listed are culled out of individual responses of farmers to the Questionnaire and further discussions in the form of personal interviews.

Secondly at the intermediate Stage, Storage and Spoilage of crops due to lack of Storage facilities continued to be a major problem for farmers in Gujarat. Farmers pack in bags or in local cases made of iron or wet sand, but quality of storage packing is poor, so losss of 10 to 20%. Farmers say that Godown facilities are not provided by Government. If provided, it is too far and not trustworthy.

As far as irrigation is concerned we can say that large farmers having some ability to ensure storage of water in Kheda and Vadodara falling in catchment areas of Sardar Sarovar have become more prosperous. The situation of small farmers has also improved due to excess flood waters and catchment area of Mahi Canal in these two districts. As far as the rest of the study area is concerned in Saurashtra and rocky areas of Panchmahal, the impact of Narmada is not yet felt. Irrigation till recently was by digging borewells and electric tube wells, canal irrigation through Sardar Sarovar has led to demand for electricity for irrigation declining.

Electric tube wells are the major source of irrigation; in some areas, irrigation is done by diesel tube wells and bore wells as well. This shows that there is sufficient supply of electricity for irrigation. Our sample shows that investment in tube wells is high. There is a great thirst for water in Gujarat agriculture and this continues with SSP water. Some farmers, specially large farmers withy borewell sell water at the rate of ₹ 40 to ₹ 50 per hour for 2 to 6 hours or more.

Prosperity has led to use of threshers, tractors and tube wells, migrant labour is not easily available due to MNREGA and family hands not available due to family members going to foreign countries,so machine becomes substitute. However Threshers and Tractors are either provided on rent by migrant farmers from Punjab or are available by rich farmers, for instance Patel farmer in Anand District.

Maintaining cattle/buffalo is not a viable proposition for the smaller farms, as their use has become extremely confined in the face of competition from tractors under modern cultivation practices. Livestock and fodder prices are also inflating. Across all size classes, livestock other than cattle/buffalo is not kept, as the average number of ruminants is quite low which confirms their prohibitive costs. Across farm sizes, apart from small farms, farmer households have large per hectare cattle holding since dairying is a major source of livelihood. Livestock per household in large farms is very high; this is a feature which results naturally in societies where number of cattle owned is seen as a sign of wealth. Junagadh and Banaskantha specially see Animal Husbandry.

Major output consequences are in medium and large farms; taking the agricultural year as a whole, wheat emerges in quantity terms as the largest crop. This is noteworthy because cereals were falling as a proportion of Gujarat agriculture in earlier decades. SSP has led to this reversal. The next story is cotton which is the powerful story of a technology-led star performance. The falling importance of oil seeds comes out. The medium and large farmers are the main actors in Gujarat's agricultural performance. Wheat in Kheda and Junagadh, Bajra in Banaskantha and Cotton as a supplementary crop in Junagadh, Banaskantha and Kheda are generally grown.

As far as Sale of Crop is concerned, The major feature which emerge is the better terms received in the market by medium and large farmers. The impression that in Gujarat cooperative institutions lead to improved terms for small and marginal farms is not borne out by this study. Sales are generally to private trader/money lender and increase monotonically by size.

A greater proportion (60%) of farmers sell in local market across farm sizes. However around 40 per cent of households sell in distant markets. The farmer generally prefers local market. Also the average transport cost per quintal is highest for large farms. The average distance to market is around 10 kms. Around 40% of farmers do not sell in local market farmers are willing to travel around 10 km and spend 10 to 17 rs per quintal on transport.

Unlike Punjab and Haryana, only less than a quarter are aware of government minimum support price, traders are more important than government agencies, though a market based agriculture, incremental sale possibilities and factors like future trading are not very dominant.

FCI or Government Procurement is absent due to inconvenience to farmer, FCI does Goal Based procurement, often it only buys till a certain quantity, there are quite often deals which are stuck with local dalals, plus FCI staff can be quite demanding, trader is in direct contact with farmer, though farmer fears exploitation, but is still familiar with the trader who buys the crop at the field conveniently.

Crop losses are generally attained during harvesting. Interestingly, small farmers have a significant proportion of losses. It should also be mentioned here that crop loss in harvesting depends much upon factors like the state of maturity of crops, timing of harvesting, unwanted rainfall in the maturity period, distance of plot from farmhouse, etc.

Crop losses occur during transport of crop output. This happens mainly during transporting harvested crop from field to threshing floor and transporting stored crop from farm to market. Losses are generally attained while transporting through tractor that being the dominant mode of transportation. Some losses are also attained while transporting by person on head, as well as by animal. Losses in packing are during packing in bags.

Credit

Generally larger farmers are aware about credit. The institutional sources of credit are more dominant like banks and cooperative societies. Half of the medium farms and three quarters of large farms have access to credit. The average amount of loan is around ₹ 1.5 lakh. Getting a loan from bank is not difficult.

The medium and large farmers are more networked, communication helps them more. By and large, the trader acts as a source of information, though media is also available.

Conclusion

Development of efficient agricultural marketing is crucial for accelerating the growth of agricultural production and marketed surplus. An efficient marketing system must ensure best possible return for sale of produce. The investigation reveals that food grains market is highly dominated by private sector and traders were observed to exploit producers in the absence of an organised dissemination of market information. The study reveals that majority households were lacking marketing intelligence. Majority of households were receiving information from traders regarding the market. The study illustrated that total production losses at different stages of handling were high. By minimising the losses at different stages, marketed surplus and financial benefits to producers can be enhanced. For minimisation of losses, technical backup and support with regard to scientific storage, use of mechanical operations at harvesting stages, and mode of packing and transportation should be disseminated. Moreover, creation of proper and adequate storage facilities at producers' level will reduce the storage losses and enhance the bargaining power of producers in the marketing of produce, which will create positive impact on their net profitability.

A regression study done in the project indicates that factors representing developed agriculture have a significant effect on the marketed surplus ratio. Distance to Market, Non Farm Income, Awareness of MSP, Access to Credit, Education, Inputs like Tractors, Tubewells, Cattle are significantly determining the marketed amount. Accordingly a Production function determined by Commercialisation and Market linkages and networking including modern inputs and credit is seen to operate.